# Grandma & Grandpa's

# BIG
# BOOK
## Of
# FUN

# Grandma
# & Grandpa's
# BIG BOOK
# *Of* FUN

## Great things to make
## and do with grandkids

**Jean Luttrell**
*Illustrations by Chuck Luttrell*

**Marlor Press, Inc.**
**Saint Paul, MN**

# Grandma & Grandpa's Big Book Of Fun

**Published by**
**Marlor Press, Inc.**

**Copyright 2001 by Jean Luttrell**

Illustrations by Chuck Luttrell

Cover design by Mighty Media

Printed in the United States of America

ISBN 1-892147-05-x

Distributed to the book trade by
Independent Publishers Group, Chicago

**MARLOR PRESS, INC.**
4304 Brigadoon Drive
Saint Paul, MN 55126

*To Jessica Elizabeth Luttrell*

*February 20, 1981 –*
*November 15, 1999*

# TABLE OF CONTENTS

## Chapter 3    Let the games begin!
*Indoor and outdoor games*

*Chapter 4* **What can we do?**
*Suggestions for doing
things together*

**Chapter 5** **Let's make something!**
*Directions for making gifts, toys and decorations*

*Chapter 6*   **Let's Celebrate!**
*Suggestions for
special days and holidays*

# Welcome to Grandma and Grampa's house

WHETHER YOUR GRANDCHILD or grandchildren live miles away or just around the corner, whether your house is an exciting vacation destination or an interesting stop-off for after school visits, you need things – lots of things – for him or her to do. This book is your answer to "What's there to do?"

To establish a warm, loving relationship with your grandchild, take the initiative — invite the child to come for a visit.

True, you can enjoy grandchildren in their home, but

this is no substitute for entertaining them at *your* house.

Think about it – could grandma invade her daughter-in-law's bedroom in search of dresses, jewelry and make-up to put on a fashion show?

Clear a date and time for the visit with the adults involved, then pick up the phone and say something like, "Hi, Tammy. It's Grandma, and I was wondering if you would like to visit Disneyland with Grandma and Grandpa this year?"

Or, "Hi, Bobby. Would you like to come for a visit this summer? Grandpa has been talking about building a tree house in that old apple tree in the back yard. He could use some help."

Be **enthusiastic**! Mention a special event you've planned. Is there an amusement park in your area? Is a circus coming to town? How about an old fashioned Fourth of July picnic?

## Helpful hints

❑ *When entertaining a very young child, invite the entire family.*

❑ *Children under the age of six do not take well to being separated from Mommy.*

❑ *To avoid homesickness the first visit should be no longer than three days.*

# 1
# Getting Ready

NOW YOUR GRANDCHILD or grandchildren are coming and you'd better be ready. This means get plenty of rest before they arrive and plan *various* activities for each day of their stay.

But, be ready to adapt and incorporate your grandchildren's ideas. Use this book as a resource for planning activities. Add to these suggestions. Your grandchild will probably have some terrific ideas too.

If when you invited your grandchild you said you would go to Disneyland or some other major attraction, do that first. Children are impatient. You won't want to hear "When are we going to Disneyland?" a dozen times a day every day.

Anyway it's a good idea to start the visit off with a bang and also end with a special event.

To get ready, you'll want to accumulate some basic supplies and materials.

## Supplies & materials

❑ Lined and unlined plain paper
❑ Construction paper in a variety of colors
❑ Colored pencils, water-soluble markers, and crayons
❑ Water-soluble paint
❑ Non-toxic child-safe glue
❑ Sequins and stickers
❑ Blunt-nose scissors
❑ Paintbrushes
❑ Clear plastic mending tape, duct tape
❑ String
❑ Clear plastic wrap

If you look around, you can find a number of fun things to play with. Here are some ideas.

❑ Look in the attic or garage for old toys.
❑ Go to yard sales and purchase items suitable for your grandchild's age.
❑ Puzzles (less than 100 pieces), books, games and other toys can often be found in yard sales.
❑ Collect boxes from as small as a matchbox to as large as a refrigerator box. (See Chapter 2)
❑ Save your old party dresses, hats, high-heel shoes, purses and jewelry in a box or laundry basket for the little girl who wants to play dress-up.
❑ Don't forget to put men's coats, ties and hats in the box. Boys like to dress-up too.

---

### Helpful hint

*Do not let your grandchild do something he or she is absolutely forbidden to do at home. If you do, the child will probably not be allowed to visit you again.*

---

## Parent's rules

Ask the parents about their rules. That way, you'll be certain to know what is practiced in your grandchild's household.

❑ Is your grandchild allergic to anything?

❑ What about videos and TV programs? Which ones are okay and which ones are forbidden?

❑ Are there foods your grandchild is not allowed to eat?

❑ What time is the usual bedtime?

Okay, so grandparents bend the rules sometimes!

## Ask the kids, too

Kids will tell you exactly what they like and what they don't like. You just have to ask.

One grandchild will love to pretend. Another child will think pretend games are silly.

Be prepared to make suggestions. Be enthusiastic!

Say something like, "I've got a box of party dresses upstairs. Let's go try them on! We could put on a fashion show for Grandpa!"

Or, "How about a game? Grandpa thinks he can beat us. What do you think?"

## First visit

For the first visit, be certain to plan a variety of things to do. These can be pretend plays, games (both indoor and outdoor), things to make and things to do together. You'll find lots of ideas in this book.

What about the child who lives close and drops in two or three times a week? (Now this is what I call an ideal situation.) You can be much more relaxed, because you

know what the child likes – which games to play and which cookies to keep in the cookie jar.

You can find new activities in this book and plan a few surprises – especially at holiday times.

Sometimes using your imagination and being flexible and enthusiastic will not carry the day – or the grandchild. (That's when you'll need a good sense of humor.)

But in the end the benefits of entertaining a grandchild in your home outweigh the problems and you (and your grandchild) will have memories to last a lifetime.

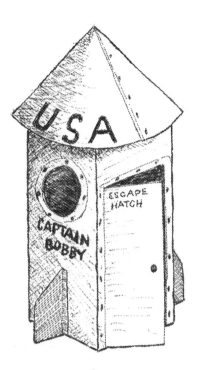

# 2
# Let's Pretend!

### Fun with a box

TO A CHILD, boxes are lots of fun. With a little imagination, a big box can become: ❑a space ship ❑ a playhouse ❑a puppet theater ❑or whatever your grandchild thinks it should be.

Large boxes are not that hard to find. Many things come in big boxes – washing machines, dryers, water heaters, tables and chairs and refrigerators – to name a few. **Don't throw those boxes away.**

If you don't have a big box you can always ask the manager of an appliance store, a contractor or a plumber to save a box for you.

Give a child a box or two and a roll of duct tape and he or she will play for hours. Don't waste your money on a plastic playhouse or fort. They look nice, but the child can't cut a new hole for a window in a plastic house. It can't be painted a new color. It can't be remodeled.

But a *box!* A creative child can do anything with a box.

### How to build a space ship

**Materials:** 1 large box, water-soluble paints, tagboard and duct tape.

**Optional Materials:** Spray paint, clear plastic wrap.

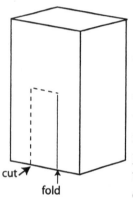

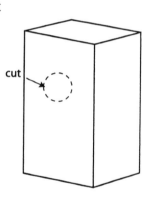

❑ Place the box in an upright postion. Cut across the center and down to the bottom of the box. Fold back to make the hatch.

❑Cut a round hole at the child's eye level in the front of the box to make a porthole. Clear plastic wrap may be taped inside the box to cover the hole.

❑ Tape cardboard tail fins to the bottom of the box.

❑ Add a nose cone made of tagboard.

### Add a nose cone

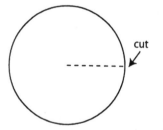

❑ Cut a large circle out of tagboard.

❑ Mark center and cut from edge to center.

❑ Overlap cut edges and tape or staple to form cone.

❑ Paint. Let grandchild choose the color. Brave grandparents may allow the child to use spray paint.

## How to make a space helmet

**Materials:** Large paper grocery sack.

**Optional Materials:** Water-soluble paint, clear plastic wrap, tape.

❑ Place the sack over the child's head and mark the area in front of his or her face.

❑ Remove sack and cut a round hole the size of the child's face.

❑ Make U-shaped cuts in the sides of the sack to fit over child's shoulders.

❑ (Optional) Paint outside of sack to match space ship and tape clear plastic wrap over the face hole on the inside of the sack.

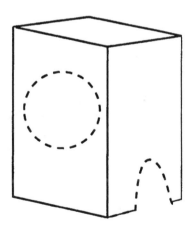

Paper sack space helmet

## Blast off!

Your grandchild stands inside the space ship and you count down to blast off. Make engine noises. Shake the space ship to simulate lift off.

**Warning:** *Do not lift the space ship. Remember this is all pretend. A real lift-off could send Grandpa to the hospital instead of putting the grandchild into orbit.*

On the trip through space there are many asteroids, which must be dodged.

(Shake the space ship as it dodges asteroids.)

After a safe moon landing don space helmets and go for a walk on the moon.

Take along plastic bags for moon rocks (specimens to be brought back to Earth).

Remember the moon's gravitational pull is not as great as Earth's so take big bouncing steps as you explore the moon's surface.

Repeat the trip to the moon until you or your child tires of the game. With each successive trip the asteroids can increase and the shaking maneuvers to avoid asteroids become more violent. This makes the trip more fun.

Back on Earth, take the moon specimens to **Grandma's Space Museum** for classification – big, small, black, red, strange, ordinary – and display.

You might want to save rocks with interesting shapes for rock decorating. (See Chapter 5)

## How to make a playhouse

**Materials:** A big box, water-soluble paint, duct tape.

❑ Cut off one side of the box.
❑ Tape the open end shut.
❑ With cut-off side up, make an L-shaped cut from the top to the bottom (floor) and about 18 inches along the bottom.
❑ Fold this section back to make a door.
❑ Paint windows on the sides of the box.
❑ Paint flowers growing beside the house.
❑ Furnish the house with smaller boxes for stove, table, cupboards and doll beds.
❑ With the house finished and furnished, you and your grandchild are ready to play with dolls or perhaps serve tea.

Cut along dotted line.

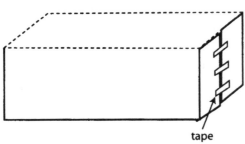

tape

**Have a tea party**

Bake cookies, make some fruit punch, set the table with a few of your old dishes, and you and your grandchild can have a tea party. Dolls and stuffed animals may be invited to the party.

**A fun puppet theater**

You can put on a puppet show. All it takes is a stage, which you easily can make out of a box, plus some paper-bag hand puppets.

**Materials**: a large cardboard box.

❑ Place box in an upright position.

❑ Cut a large window in the front of the box near the top.

❑ Cut away the bottom half of the back side.

To put on a puppet show, kneel or sit inside the box and hold puppets in the window facing out toward the audience (Grandma or Grandpa) in front.

The puppet stage can be dressed up with curtains made

from old towels or large scraps of material. Hang curtains on a string fastened across the top of the box. Scenery can be painted on a large sheet of paper taped across the back of the stage.

Choose a story to dramatize or make up your own story. (Simple well-known stories with few characters are easiest to dramatize.)

### Make paper-bag puppets

**Materials:** Sack-lunch-size paper bags, colored paper, crayons or markers, glue.

❑ Glue colored paper or use crayons or markers to make a face on the bottom of a sack-lunch-size bag.

❑ Make the mouth at the bottom so that your characters will appear to talk when your hand inside the bag is opened and closed.

❑ Use the large-box-puppet theater described above for a stage, or kneel behind a sofa or couch and use the top of the sofa for a stage.

### Stick puppets

**Materials:** Unsharpened pencils or 12 inch rulers, paper, crayons, old magazines, Scotch tape.

❑ Draw, color (or find pictures in magazines) and cut out characters.

Fasten puppet characters to unsharpened pencils or 12-inch rulers with Scotch tape.

❑ Put on puppet show.

## Have an elegant fashion show

**Materials:** Grandma's old party dresses, hats, shoes, jewelry and cosmetics.

### Preparations

❑ Apply make-up.
❑ Try on various combinations of dresses, hats and shoes.
❑ Select appropriate jewelry.

With Grandpa as captive audience your grandchild models while Grandma ad-libs or reads from cue cards a description of each outfit. You should point out that these are the latest creations from Paris; mention the matching colors and tell where each might be worn — such as, "Suitable for an evening at the White House with the President and First Lady."

## Beauty parlor

**Materials:** Comb, hairbrush, curlers, water spray bottle, nail polish.

Brave grandmothers become customers at granddaughter's beauty shop. Here, hair is styled by a creative beautician. Results vary according to the child's age and degree of talent. Be prepared for a surprising hair-do!

And why not get a manicure as well?

## Build a play store

**Materials:** Table or box for counter, shelves for display, paper, colored markers, canned goods, food boxes and plastic containers from Grandma's pantry.

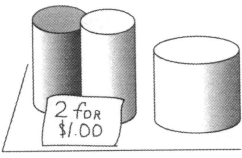

## Preparations

❑ Use paper and colored markers to make play money – bills and coins – in each denomination.

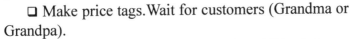

❑ Arrange canned goods on shelves.

❑ Make price tags. Wait for customers (Grandma or Grandpa).

After playing pretend store an older child might want to have a real store – a lemonade stand (See Chapter 4).

## Play school

**Materials:** A small blackboard, chalk, a yardstick.

**Optional Materials:** Old school books, paper, pencils, school bell.

## Preparations

❑ Place blackboard in front of chairs for students.

❑ Have books, paper and pencils on hand for written assignments.

Your grandchild is the teacher and you, dolls and stuffed animals are the not too smart pupils. The teacher directs operations here – writing on the blackboard, rapping for order with the yardstick and barking out directions.

### Road construction

**Materials:** Toy tractors, bulldozers (these can be your children's old toys or yard sale purchases) and a sandbox or dirt area.

❑ Get down on your hands and knees in the sand or dirt and follow your grandchild's lead.
❑ Make motor noises when pushing truck or bulldozer and remember to beep a warning when backing up.
❑ Dig ditches, build bridges, haul rocks.

### Build a play farm

Because tractors, bulldozers and trucks have replaced horses on farms, this pretend game can be an extension road construction.

**Materials:** Toys used for road construction, empty milk cartons, empty saltbox, construction paper, grass seed.

While playing road construction you might suggest making a farm. Say something like, "Why don't you bring your bulldozer over here to make a smooth place so we can plant grass and make a farm?"

❑ Clear and level a small dirt area. Add water to make a moist seed bed. Sprinkle grass seeds. Cover seeds with a thin layer of dirt. Gently sprinkle with water every day. In about a week, the farm will have a field of green grass.

❑ While waiting for grass to grow, use bulldozers and trucks to dig ponds and make roads.

❑ Milk cartons can be painted or covered with construction paper to make a house and barn.

❑ Turn a saltbox or round oatmeal box into a silo with a cone shaped top cut from construction paper.

## How to make fences

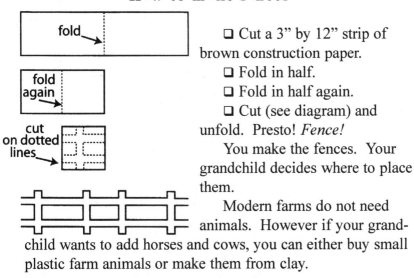

❑ Cut a 3" by 12" strip of brown construction paper.

❑ Fold in half.

❑ Fold in half again.

❑ Cut (see diagram) and unfold. Presto! *Fence!*

You make the fences. Your grandchild decides where to place them.

Modern farms do not need animals. However if your grandchild wants to add horses and cows, you can either buy small plastic farm animals or make them from clay.

## Put on a back yard circus

All you need are a back yard and two or more grandchildren or neighborhood kids with lively imaginations. Place a garden hose on the ground in a circle and you have a circus ring. Now you need circus acts. For starters, how about a clown, a dancing horse and a gymnast? Your kids will have more ideas. Don't forget the ringmaster!

### Ringmaster

**Costume:** A man's black coat, a top hat and a whip.

Grandpa can supply the black coat (any dark color coat will do). If you don't have a top hat, try taping black construction paper around the crown of an old felt hat. A whip can be made by tying string or twine to a short straight stick.

### Be a clown

**Costume:** Your creative grandchild will be sure to find a proper clown outfit in your box of dress-up clothes. A painted face is optional.

You won't need to suggest acts for the clown. Kids are natural clowns. If necessary remind him or her that a clown runs into things, stumbles, falls down, and mimics. Your clown is sure to come up with some outrageous acts. Outrageous is okay, but quickly put a stop to any act that is dangerous.

### Dancing horse

**Costume materials:** Two large paper grocery sacks, paint, tape, construction paper, a broom, old sheet or blanket.

❑ Make two cuts on the fold in a large grocery sack. Starting at the top cut halfway to the bottom of the sack.

❑ Push the bottom of the uncut sack into the hole cut in

the side of the other sack and fasten with tape or glue. This makes the horse's head.

❑ Paint eyes, mouth and nose. Tape or glue ears cut from construction paper on the sack.

❑ Tape the horse head onto a broom.

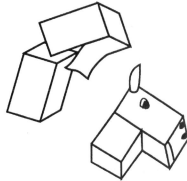

Two kids stand, one behind the other. Front child holds the broom with head attached to make the front part of the horse. The second child stoops over, places his or her hands on the front child's waist and his or her head against the first child's back to make the horse's rear.

Cover the two children with a sheet or blanket. Use safety pins to secure the cover.

Put a record on the record player or a CD in the CD player and let the dancing horse prance around the ring, bob its head, kick up its heels, wiggle its behind and do things no horse ever did.

## Gymnast

Put an old mattress on the ground and let your future Olympian strut her or his stuff.

Grandkids perform. Grandparents applaud.

## Create your own play

**Materials:** A box of dress-up clothes, clothesline rope or twine, sheet or old blanket.

Hang an old sheet or blanket on rope or twine tied between two porch posts and you have a stage. If you don't have an old fashioned front porch try curtaining off a corner of the garage or one side of a room.

Your grandkids can now act out a familiar fairytale or make up a story about a favorite storybook character. You can jump start their imaginations by saying something like, "What would **Pippi Longstocking** do if she were here right now visiting her grandparents?" Or, "Suppose **Harry Potter** were living right here in this town, in this house. What do you think he would be doing?" Some children will want to write a script, but most kids prefer extemporaneous action.

Children only need a stage, a costume and an uncritical audience. They love to perform.

### Be a rock star

PRESENTING
TAMMY JONES

**Materials:** Box of dress-up clothes, an improvised stage, a record, tape or CD player.

**Optional accessory:** Microphone. Make a microphone by gluing black construction paper around a toilet paper tube or paper towel tube. Tape a few feet of string or twine to the end of the tube for the cord.

Let your grandchild dress-up in a long swishy dress, put on a record or turn on tape or CD player and you will be entertained (or amused.)

### Dancer

**Materials:** Box of dress-up clothes, improvised stage, record, tape or CD player.

**Optional accessory:** Tambourine.

**Materials for tambourine:** 2 paper plates, dry beans or small pebbles, glue or stapler, hole punch, ribbon or yarn, paint, glitter.

**Optional material:** Small sleigh bells.

❑ Put a few dry beans or small pebbles on a paper plate.
❑ Glue or staple the second paper plate on top.
❑ Punch holes with paper punch around the edge and lace

the two plates together with ribbon or yarn.

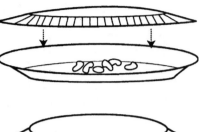

❑ (Optional) For real tambourine jiggle thread a few small sleigh bells on the ribbon or yarn lacing.

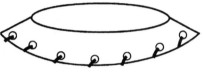

❑ Decorate with paint and glitter.

Turn on the music. Your talented grandkid will know what to do.

## How to put on a magic show

You pretend to be a magician. It's not difficult, especially if you practice your tricks in advance.

**Materials:** Deck of cards, small drinking glass, thin thread, pencil.

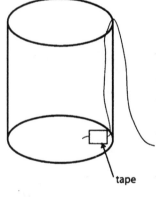

Tape thread to glass

❑ Before your audience arrives, use transparent tape to tape a thin light-colored thread to the bottom, inside of a drinking glass. The glass should be wide enough to hold a deck of cards but not too tall.

❑ Place the glass on a table. Audience (grandchildren) should be seated eight feet or more from the table. (This trick depends on their not being able to see the thread.)

❑ Approach your audience with a deck of cards and ask a child to select a card.

❑ Walk back to the table. Place the deck, minus the card that was selected, in the glass. Say, "Remember that card. Don't let me see it."

❑ Next retrieve the selected card, hold it up where your grandchild can see it, but keep it turned away from you. Say,

Thread lifts card

"Keep your eyes on this card. Remember what card you picked."

❑Return to the table. While moving the card back and forth above the deck with one hand to attract attention to it, deftly move the thread in the glass up and over the deck of cards with the other hand.

❑Without looking at the card insert it in the deck, push the thread down with the card. Tap the top of the deck, make sure the selected card is pushed all the way to the bottom of the glass and the top is even with the other cards in the deck.

❑Wave the magic wand (a pencil) with your right hand and say, "Rise! Rise! I command Bobby's card to rise!" All eyes will be on the wand hand, allowing you to pull the thread unnoticed with your left hand. The thread under the selected card lifts it up and out of the deck.

Part of the fun will come when you show how the magic was preformed. Let your grandchild practice the trick, so he or she can amaze Mom and Dad. If a grandchild is interested in learning more tricks, look for magic books in the children's section of your library.

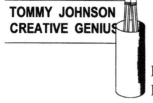

TOMMY JOHNSON
CREATIVE GENIUS

## Be a creative genius

**Materials:** Small table or desk, pencils, crayons, markers or colored pencils, paper — lined and unlined, graph paper, 12-inch ruler, scissors.

If you have a home office, set up your grandchild's work area near your desk. Now you can work together.

Your grandchild is the Creative Genius and you are the Assistant Creative Genius. Here are some ideas. Your grandchild is sure to have his or her own ideas.

### Be a new car designer

A major car company has given your grandchild a contract to produce a design for the **car of the future.** Together you will draw futuristic cars, compare results and make suggestions. Your grandchild is the **Creative Genius.** You are the assistant – the "yes-man." Praise your grandchild's designs and help to select the best ones. Tape award-winning designs on the office wall.

### Dress designer

Your grandchild has been asked to design gowns for several actresses to wear to the **Oscar Awards.** Working together you will create clothes that are unbelievably glamorous. If you are a cleaver seamstress you might offer to help your child convert one of the designs into an outfit for a Barbie Doll. But don't try something that would be too difficult – this is play, not work.

### Architect

Your young engineer is planning to build a **playhouse** or a **fort**. First he or she must make a plan. Use graph paper to make a blueprint.

Or maybe, your creative genius has been commissioned to plan a vacation house for a very rich client. Draw, discuss, compare and, above all, praise.

### Sports writer

You and your grandchild cover the local Little League **ball game** or write a report of a game watched on TV. The sports writer produces a rough draft of the big game. You, the editor with the aid of a typewriter or computer, turn his or her smudged copy into clean perfect prose.

## Newspaper editor

Why not publish your own newspaper? Your grandchild is the editor. You are the assistant editor. Write up the family and neighborhood news. Create startling headlines. Make up interesting classified ads. Draw cartoons. The newspaper can be copied (printed) at your local copy center at a very reasonable price. Send your grandchild's newspaper to Mom and Dad. They will be amazed!

## Author & illustrator

Perhaps your grandchild will want to write and illustrate **his or her own book**. You become editor and publisher. Type a few lines of the young author's story on each of several pages. Staple the pages together to make a book. Let the author illustrate his or her book.

Whatever career your grandchild chooses, don't forget to make business cards. Cut index cards to size — 3½ by 2 inches. Decorate with a logo. Be sure to include full name, title and

**Davy Wilson**
Super Architec
&
Creative Genius
116 Grandma Place
Anytown, USA

address. With a computer or typewriter you and your grandchild can make professional-looking cards.

## LAST WORDS

Some children love to pretend and this chapter and their own imaginations contain all the activities they need.

However, some children think pretend games are silly. If you are not making a hit with "Let's Pretend," turn quickly to the next chapter and "Let the Games Begin."

# 3
# Let the games begin!

### Indoor games

#### Play fun card games

**Materials:** One standard deck of playing cards.

**Optional Material:** Rule book, such as *Hoyle's Rules of Games* or *According to Hoyle.*

With a deck of cards, you can entertain any age (from 2 to 102). A two-year-old can play a game of match colors and suits. Say, "I've got an eight. Can you find an eight?"

Very young children always win! So remember to say with enthusiasm, "That's right! You win!"

At about age six, you can introduce simple games such as Fish, Old Maid or War.

## Concentration

**Materials:** One deck of playing cards.
**Number of players:** Two.

This game is played with half a deck – all of any two suits.

Lay cards face down in four rows of six cards each and one row of two cards.

The first player turns up any two cards. If they are the same denomination, the player keeps the cards and takes another turn. If the cards do not match, he or she returns them to their original position and the second player takes his or her turn.

Each time a card is turned, both players try to remember it for future turns – hence the name Concentration.

The player with the most cards at the end of the game wins.

## Dominoes

**Materials:**  Set of Double Twelve dominoes.
**Optional Material:** *Hoyle's Rules of Games* or *According to Hoyle* or directions included with the dominoes for playing various games.

Set a toddler down, get out the dominoes and play. Build towers, make trains and line 'em up and knock 'em down. With older children you can play any number of other domino games described in the box.

## Jax

This old-fashioned game is still available for less than a dollar in the toy departments of most variety stores.

**Materials:** Set of Jax (eight jax and a small ball).

Sit on the floor and scatter the jax in front of you. Using only one hand, bounce the ball, pick up a jax and catch the ball. Simple! But the game gets harder. After all jax are picked up, one at a time, you scatter them again and pick them up two at a time while the ball bounces once. Each time you play, you increase the number of jax picked up by one. Try picking up *eight* scattered jax while the ball bounces only once!

> **Warning:** Do not let young children play with Jax or any other small game pieces that might cause choking.

## Jack straws

**Materials:** Set of Jack Straws or 15 or more drinking straws.

Hold straws in one hand about 1 foot from the playing surface. Drop the straws. Players try to remove one straw from the pile without disturbing any of the others. If a straw other than the one selected moves, the player loses his or her turn. However, if the player removes a straw without moving any others, he or she takes another turn. Each player keeps the straws he or she removed. When all straws are picked up, the person with the most straws wins the game.

## Old- fashioned board games

In the game department of your local toy store, you will find dozens of boxed games all conveniently marked with appropriate ages of players.

### Checkers

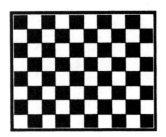

**Materials:** Set of checkers, a checkerboard.

**Optional Material:** *Hoyle's Rules of Games* or *According to Hoyle.*

Directions for playing are usually included with the board and checkers. However, this seemingly easy game is really quite complex. If an older grandchild takes a serious interest in this game (wants to beat Grandpa), he or she should study *Hoyle's.*

### Aggravation

**Materials:** Four-player Aggravation game.

People have been playing this game for many years and in its various forms it has been called everything from Wahoo to Aggravation.

It's our family's favorite game, because even though some strategy is involved, winning depends mainly on luck – the roll of the dice. This element of luck makes it possible for the youngest player to beat Grandpa, the super strategist.

## MINIMAL EQUIPMENT GAMES

These games can be time fillers for those moments when you have to wait for someone or something.

### Tic-Tac-Toe

winner

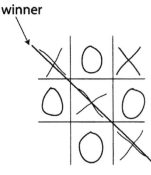

**Materials:** Pencil, paper.
**Number of players:** Two

❑ Draw four lines to make a grid.
❑ A player starts the game by putting his mark – an X or an O – in a square on the grid. Take turns.
❑ The first player to have three marks in a row (vertically, horizontally or diagonally) wins the game.

### Hangman

GRANDMA

**Materials:** Pencil, paper.
**Number of players:** Two.

❑ One player thinks of a word and makes a dash for each letter in the word.
❑ The other player guesses a letter.
❑ If the letter is in the word, it is placed on the appropriate dash. If the letter is not in the word, a section of a gallows is drawn on the paper. After a simple scaffold (three lines) is drawn, a wrong guess results in a body part (head, body, arms, legs) being added to the drawing.
❑ The player continues to guess letters until he or she either spells the word or is hanged.

## I'm thinking

This guessing game can be varied with ground rules from easy (something you can see) to difficult (anything you can think of).

**Materials:** None.
**Number of players:** Two or more.

❑ One person thinks of a person, place or thing.

❑ The players ask questions that can be answered by yes or no.

❑ If the answer is guessed in twenty questions or less, the person guessing correctly is the winner and the leader of the next game.

## Simon Says

**Number of players:** Two or more.
**Materials:** None.

The leader gives orders by saying, "Simon says _____." The players do only those things Simon tells them to do.

You might say, "Simon says jump up." Each player would jump up and then wait for the next command.

After several "Simon says" directions, the leader gives an order without the words "Simon says." Anyone following this direction is out of the game.

This game can be played in a car while traveling by having Simon give instructions for things you can do with your hands, such as, "Simon says thumbs up."

## Scissors, paper, stone

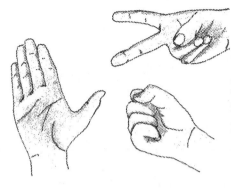

**Materials:** None.
**Number of players**:  Two.

❑ Both players hold one hand behind their backs and make it into a **scissors** (two fingers spread apart in a V); a **paper** (hand held palm up and flat); or **stone** (hand curled into a fist).

❑ Count together "one, two, three," then simultaneously show a scissors, paper or stone.

❑ Compare:

Both players the same; no winner.

Scissors and paper; scissors wins because scissors cut paper.

Stone and paper; paper wins because paper wraps stone.

Stone and scissors; stone wins because stone blunts scissors.

## ACTIVE INDOORS GAMES

It's raining and cold outside. Your grandchild is overflowing with energy and cannot sit still. Now is the time for some active indoor games.

### Hide the Thimble

**Materials:**  Grandma's thimble.

One person hides the thimble while other players are in another room. After the thimble has been partially concealed, the players search for it. As the player approaches the thimble, say, "Getting warmer." When a player moves away from area where thimble is hidden say, "Getting colder." The finder hides the thimble for the next game.

## Tissue paper and straw race

**Materials:** Soft-drink-size straws, tissue paper.

**Preparation:** Cut small circles (about 2 inches in diameter) of tissue paper. Make six of these disks for each player.

❑ Place the tissue paper disks on one side of the room and bowls at the opposite side.

❑ Give each player a straw. Instruct players to pick up and keep the tissue paper on the end of the straw by sucking (creating a partial vacuum).

❑ Players race to see who can move all their tissue paper disks from the starting line to the bowl first. Touching disks with hands is not allowed.

## Mother, may I?

**Materials:** None.

**Players:** Three or more. Three, four and five-year olds love this game.

The leader, "Mother," stands at one end of the room and players stand at the other end, or better yet, across the room and down the hall.

The players take turns asking if they may take a certain number and type of steps. They must begin their request by saying, "Mother may I…" Since the object of the game is to reach "Mother," players who fail to use the words, "Mother may I" or ask for too many steps are told, "No, you may not."

The first player to reach "Mother" becomes the leader for the next game.

## Hide and seek

**Materials:** None.
**Number of players:** Two.

You can play this game in the house with very young grandkids. One, two and three-year-olds hide in the same place over and over. As you pretend to look for them, remember to say something like, "Where's Bobby? Now where could he be hiding?" Then squeal in surprise when you look under the table (or wherever he's hiding) and suddenly find him.

**Helpful hint:** Don't play hide and seek indoors with older grandkids. Big kids can cause big damage to house and furniture.

## Charades

**Materials:** None.

The leader chooses a word or phrase, which can be acted out. Players watch the action and guess. The player guessing the answer thinks of the next word or phrase.

## Box hockey

**Materials:** Large flat cardboard box, duct tape, button, two Popsicle sticks.

Before you play this game you will need to make a box-hockey rink.

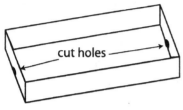

❑ Select either the top or bottom of a large flat cardboard box, such as a coat box.

❑ Cut a small hole at the bottom, near the center, in each end of the box. The hole must be large enough to allow the button (puck) to pass through easily.

❑ Measure and cut a piece of cardboard to fit across the center of the box.

❑ Cut two small holes at the bottom of this hockey-rink divider.

❑ Tape the divider securely across the center of the box.

❑ Tape a small cardboard launch pad on top, center of the divider.

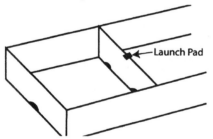

This game gets wild, so reinforce sides and divider with lots of duct tape. Now you are ready to play the game!

**Number of players:** Two.

❑ Players hold Popsicle sticks (hockey sticks) and sit or kneel on each side of the box. Place the button (hockey puck) on the launch pad.

❑ Count: "Hockey one," touch sticks over the puck; "Hockey two," touch sticks; "Hockey three!" This time after touching sticks the players go after the button.

❑ Button can only be moved with sticks and can only be transferred from one side of box to the other by being pushed through one of the two holes in the divider.

❑ The first player to make a goal (push the button through the hole at the bottom of the opponent's hockey rink and out of the box) wins the game.

## Indoor basketball

**Materials:** Small indoor basketball set (These sets, which contain a small basket and a soft sponge rubber ball can be purchased in toy departments for less than $5).

Fasten basket to the top edge of a table, bookcase or door. The height of the basket depends on the height of the smallest player. Push back furniture, remove breakables and you are ready for action. How about a game of one-on-one?

If you do not have an indoor basketball set you might try improvising with a paper ball made of crushed newspaper held together with masking tape. A basket can be constructed by cutting the center out of a paper plate.

## Make flying saucers

**Materials:** Paper plates, butcher paper or vinyl table-cloth, string, felt-tip marker pen.

**Preparation**: Staple or glue two paper plates together to make a flying saucer.

Draw a circular target on butcher paper or vinyl tablecloth. Place the target on the floor on one side of a room, stand at the other side of the room and toss flying saucers into the circle. For an easier game put the target at one end of a hall, stand and toss from the other end.

**Fun with ring toss**

**Materials:** Paper plate rings, one kitchen-type chair.

**Preparation**: Cut the center out of lunch-size and dessert-size paper plates. Glue or staple the edges of two plates together. Make three rings of each size for each player.

Turn a kitchen-type chair over — back touches floor and legs stick up.

Stand back and try to toss paper plate rings over a chair leg. Each player is allowed three tosses with big (lunch-size plate) rings and three tosses with small (dessert-size plate) rings. Adjust the distance between players and chair to match ability and age.

Score 5 points for each successful toss with big rings and 10 points for each small ring that goes over a chair leg.

## Balloon ball

**Materials:** Balloons, string.

**Number of players:** Two or more.

Move the furniture out of the way, tie a string across the center of the room about four feet from the floor and bat a balloon back and forth. Bat the balloon up as many times as necessary, but do not catch it. If the balloon touches the floor or you catch it, your opponent makes a point.

## Blow-ball

**Materials:** Straws, cotton ball, string, small table.
**Number of players:** Two.

Put a string across the center of a small table, such as a coffee table. Place a cotton ball near the center of the string. Two players move the ball by blowing on it through a straw. You score a goal by blowing the ball off your opponent's end of the table.

## Pendulum Bowling

**Materials:** 10 golf tees, string, beanbag.
**Number of players:** Two or more.
**Preparation:** Fasten a long string to the center of the facing over a doorway. Tie a beanbag on the end of the string. Shorten or lengthen the string to make a pendulum that clears the floor with less than an inch to spare. Set up golf tees (bowling pins) in the doorway.

The bowler stands on a designated spot several feet from the pins and lets the pendulum swing forward and back. One swing of the pendulum – forward and back – is a turn. Players take turns.

Score: One point for each golf tee knocked down, ten extra points for a strike. You add up the points after ten turns to see who is the winner.

## Beanbag

Make a beanbag for pendulum bowling from the foot part of an old sock. Fill the bottom of the sock with beans, tie securely and cut off the top. This is a quick, easy way to make a beanbag that can be used in a variety of games. For added security, put the beans in a plastic sandwich bag before putting them in the sock.

## Fishing Game

**Materials:** String, cardboard, paper clips, sticks for fishing poles, washtub.

**Preparation:** Draw and cut out cardboard fish. Make big ones and small ones.

❑ Write a point value on each fish.

❑ With a paper punch, make an eye in each fish.

Place a small amount of sand or gravel in the bottom of a washtub. Stand the fish upright by wedging the tails into the sand or gravel.

❑ Make fishing poles with sticks, string and bent paper-clips.

❑ Players try to catch fish by hooking the bent paperclip through the eye. Each player may have a one-minute turn.

❑ Repeat turns until all fish are caught. Player with the most points wins the game.

## OUTDOORS GAMES

## Basketball

**Materials:** Basketball, basket with backboard.

One-on-one games of basketball are action-packed fun, but here is another game that will not be so hard on the adult player.

### How to play horse

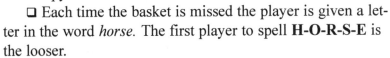

❑ The player starting the game attempts to make a basket standing or moving at a certain distance from the basket and tossing the ball in a prescribed way.

❑ The other player tries to make a basket at the same distance and in the same way.

❑ If the second player makes a basket, he or she then becomes the leader and sets up the shot, which the opponent must copy.

❑ Each time the basket is missed the player is given a letter in the word *horse*. The first player to spell **H-O-R-S-E** is the looser.

This is a good, slow-paced game that won't cause an adult to have a heart attack.

Base

X Pitcher

☐
X   X Kickers
X

### Backyard kickball

**Materials:** Soccer ball or large rubber ball.

**Number of players:** Three or more (The game requires one pitcher and, at least, two kickers.)

Kickball, a favorite schoolyard game, is played like softball but a ball is kicked instead of batted. In this backyard variation of the game, there are only two bases – home base and another at the far end of the playing area.

A square scratched in the dirt can serve as home base and a fence or tree can be the other base.

❑ The pitcher rolls the ball to the kicker at home base.

❑ The kicker kicks and runs to the base behind the pitcher (the backyard fence or tree) where he or she is safe.

❑ The next kicker does the same and the player on base runs for home.

❑ A kicker is out if he or she kicks a fly-ball, which is caught before it bounces. Also, a player is out if the pitcher touches him or her with the ball while running between bases.

When a kicker or runner is out, he or she changes places with the pitcher. The pitcher becomes the kicker.

---

**Warning:** Do not throw a ball at a runner in an attempt to put him or her out. Hitting a player with a thrown ball **is dangerous** and is **not allowed.**

---

## Four square

**Materials:** Large rubber ball, cement driveway or other smooth playing surface, chalk.

Your grandchild will probably be able to tell you how to play this game, because it is popular on school playgrounds. If you do not have four players, show your grandchild how the game can be played with only two or three people by drawing two or three 6 ft. squares. You might call it, Two Square or Three Square.

❑ One player stands in each square. Start the game by batting the ball up and into another square. The receiver must bat the ball into another player's square.

❑ Ball must be batted with hands, not caught and tossed.

❑ Ball can only bounce once in a square.

❑ Ball must land in a square, not on a line.

❑ Scoring: One point for the server if the receiver lets the ball bounce more than once or catches it. One point for the server, if the receiver cannot bat the ball into another square.

❑ One point for the receiver, if the ball lands on a line or outside the receiver's square.

❑ First player to score 21 points wins the game.

## Kick the can

**Materials:** One empty can.

❑ The player who is "it" stands on the can and counts to 100 by fives while the other players hide.

❑ When "it" sees a hider, he shouts, "I spy (name)" and races back to the can. "It" tries to kick the can before the hider kicks it.

❑ Any player unable to kick the can before "it" becomes "it" for the next game.

## Three tag games

### Wood tag

"It" chases players who are safe only when touching wood. Any player tagged when not touching wood becomes "it."

### Stoop tag

In this game players are safe when in a squatting or stooping position.

### "It" tag

"It" chases players who when tagged must place their left hand on the spot tagged and keep it there until he or she tags someone else. There is no safe zone or position.

Of course, "it" tries to tag a player on the knee, back or some part of the body that will make running awkward.

## Hopscotch

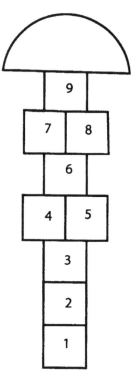

**Materials:** Chalk, a cement driveway.

Your grandchild will probably be able to show you how to play this popular playground game. But here's a refresher course:

❑ Draw a hopscotch. (See diagram.)

❑ Select a small object to use as a marker, such as a pebble.

❑ Toss marker into square number 1.

❑ Hop over the square with your marker. Hop in the next two squares, then jump with both feet landing with one foot in each of squares 4 and 5.

❑ Hop in square 6. Jump into squares 7 and 8.

❑ Hop in square 9. Step into the resting place at the end of the hopscotch.

❑ Return the same way, hoping over the square with your marker.

❑ If successful (not stepping on a line) you toss your marker into square 2 and take another turn.

You lose your turn if the marker does not land in the proper square or you step on a line. Leave marker in the square marking the last successfully completed turn. The next player must hop over the square with your marker.

The winner is the first person to reach and toss his or her marker into the resting place at the end of the hopscotch.

### Old-fashioned hopscotch

After your grandchild has shown you the modern way to play hopscotch, you might want to show him or her a game he or she won't know.

**Materials:** Chalk, a cement driveway.

With chalk draw a grid on the cement driveway. The boxes in the grid should be about one foot square.

❑ The first player hops on one foot through the entire grid. One hop in each box.

**Remember one foot only. Do not put the other foot down. Do not hop on a line.**

❑ If the player successfully completes the hopscotch grid on one foot and does not step on a line, he or she may put his or her initials in a box. This becomes the player's private spot. She or he can stand on two feet in this box and rest, but no other player can hop in this box.

❑ The second player hops in each box until he or she comes to the initialed box, which he or she must hop over (one long hop) without touching a line.

❑ If you step on a line you do not get to initial a box.

❑ Players take turns.

❑ Player with most initialed boxes wins the game.

Start

Finish

--------

**Helpful hint**: Here's a new rule to help grandparents: Mark two squares in the grid as rest areas. All players can put two feet down in the rest squares.

--------

## Hopscotch tic tac toe

**Materials:** Chalk, cement driveway.

❑ Make a grid of nine squares as you would for Tic Tac Toe.

❑ Game is played in the same way as Old Fashioned Hopscotch.

❑ Winner must have three squares initialed in a row as for Tic Tac Toe.

## Marbles

**Materials:** Bag of marbles.

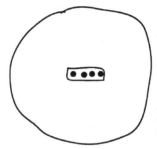

❑ Draw a circle about three feet in diameter in the dirt.

❑ Each player puts the same number of marbles on a line near the surface.

❑ Players take turns shooting (flipping a marble with his or her thumb) at a marble in the circle.

❑ A hit marble becomes the property of the shooter.

❑ The first shot is taken from the edge of the circle. Subsequent turns are shot from the spot where the marble came to rest inside the circle.

## Sponge race

**Materials:** 2 pails of water, 2 empty pails, 2 sponges, 2 cups.

**Number of players:** Two

Place two pails of water about 20 feet from the two empty pails. At a given signal, each player, carrying a cup and sponge, runs to the pail of water and fills his or her cup using the sponge. The player races back to the empty pail and pours the water into it. The action is repeated until the "time's up" signal is heard.

The player with the most water in his or her pail is the winner.

## Tin can bowling

**Materials:** One large rubber ball, 10 tin cans or plastic bottles or empty milk cartons.

Set up tin cans as you would for bowling. From a distance of about 20 ft. roll a rubber ball at the pins (cans). Each player is given two chances to knock down pins. Take turns.

Scoring: One point for each pin knocked down — ten extra points for a strike.

Winner: Player with most points after ten turns.

## Beanbag toss

**Materials**: Beanbags, chalk, sidewalk or driveway.

**Preparation:** With chalk draw a large target on the sidewalk. Write point values on the target – 20 points for a bull's-eye, 15 points for the next larger ring etc.

❑ Stand back and toss beanbags at the target.
❑ Keep track of your score.

Note: Beanbags can be made from old socks (See Pendulum Bowling).

## IMPORTANT ADVICE

❑ Games should be fun. If you or your grandchild are not having fun, stop the game and do something else.

❑ Whether teaching or learning make sure all players understand and follow the rules. (Exception: very young grandchildren make up the rules as they go along and *always win*.)

❑ Let your grandchild know (show by your behavior) that it is okay to lose. Praise good sportsmanship.

# 4

# What can we do?

## IN THE HOUSE

### Read a book

READ A BEDTIME STORY to your grandchild or your grandchild can read to you.

Either way, it undoubtedly will be an experience both of you will look back on with pleasure.

## Listen to your grandchild

These informal bedtime get-togethers on Grandma's or grandchild's bed are great for idle chit-chat. Listen. Ask questions such as: And then what happened? What did you do?

Your questions and comments let your grandchild know you are listening – really listening.

## Tell a story

Our Jess used to ask me to tell stories about when I was her age. She had favorites that she asked for over and over again.

She'd say, "Tell me about how you and Edna Lu put snowballs in a paper sack, took them to school and put them in the coat closet."

Don't worry about telling it exactly the way it happened. The truth is I can't remember what the teacher said or did when she saw a puddle of water seeping out from under the coat closet door. But when I tell the story the teacher screams and yells.

## Make shadow pictures

Before you say goodnight turn off the overhead light, take out a flashlight and make shadow pictures.

Hold the flashlight so it shines on the palm of your hand and the shadow falls on a wall. Raise and lower your little finger. Arf! Arf! A dog!

---

**Helpful hint:** Give your grandchild a flashlight to keep under his or her pillow. It's a great weapon against shadows that look like hobgoblins and things that go bump in the night.

---

You can also have fun shinning the light through your fingers. The light turns your fingers red. Try it behind your ear. Small grandchildren are amazed.

## Look at the stars

If you live where stars are clearly visible, you and your grandchild can look for planets, the Big Dipper and the Milky Way.

Grandchildren who live where pollution and city lights prevent them from seeing the moon and stars will be amazed at the way the moon moves and changes from night to night.

A current star map can be found in some newspapers in the weather section and on the Internet at: www.wunderground.com/sky/

## Draw pictures

**Materials:** Paper, crayons or colored markers or colored pencils.

Gather around the kitchen table and draw houses with the ever-present sun shinning overhead or whatever your grandchild wants to draw.

An inexpensive frame preserves and dignifies the artist's masterpiece.

### Play ring around the rosy

One and two-year-olds love to play Ring Around the Rosy. You and your toddler join and hands, move in a circle and say:

> *Ring around the rosy,*
> *Pocket full of posy,*
> *Ashes, ashes,*
> *All fall down!*

As you say the last line, you fall down. Your grandbaby will tumble to the floor, laugh and jump up ready to do it all again.

### Bake cookies

**Materials:** Things normally found in Grandma's kitchen.

For the very young grandchild, all you need are a bowl, spoon, flour, water and food coloring. Food coloring is an important ingredient in this recipe.

Set the toddler on the kitchen counter and give him or her

a bowl and spoon. Measure flour and water in a cup before dumping into the bowl.

Ask, "Is this enough flour? Is this enough water?" When well mixed, put cookies in a cold oven and bake with no heat.

Older grandchildren will want to make real cookies. Let your grand-child choose his or her favorite recipe. Grandma becomes assistant chef, cleanup crew and dishwasher.

## Cookie contest

If several grandchildren come for a visit you could have a cookie contest. Grandma and Grandpa are the judges with prizes for most original, tasti-est, prettiest, etc. Of course, everyone's a winner!

## Teach a skill

If you are a grandma or grandpa who can sew, knit, cro-chet or do simple woodcraft, you could teach an older child these skills. At our house, Grandpa has a workshop that draws our Kevin like a magnet.

He and Grandpa hammer and saw and make toy boats and airplanes that do not resem-ble anything that ever floated or flew. But they have a great time.

> **Warning:** Power tools are dangerous. **Use only hand tools.** A hand-held hammer can mash a finger, but a nail gun can put a grandparent or grandchild in the hospital.

## Put together a jigsaw puzzle

Jigsaw puzzles are great do-together projects.

Children 6 to 10 years can usually put together a 100-piece puzzle with Grandma and Grandpa's help.

Here's another puzzle:

## Tangram fun

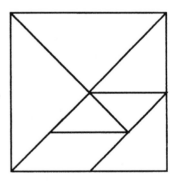

This is a tangram.

Reproduce this tangram by tracing or copying. Show your grandchild the tangram you have reproduced and tell this story in your own words:

Once upon a time there was a Chinese nobleman who had a favorite tile. (Show the tangram and tell your grandchild it represents the nobleman's tile.) One day he dropped his tile and it broke into 7 pieces. (With scissors carefully cut the tangram apart on the lines.)

The nobleman spent the rest of his life trying to put his tile back together. (Hand your grandchild the tangram pieces and let him or her try to put it back together.) It's much harder than you would think. When your grandchild gives up, show the tangram in this book and let him or her use it as a guide.

Next see what unusual shapes you and your grandchild can make with all or part of the tangram pieces.

## Grow crystals

Want to amaze your grandchild? Try growing crystals.

**Materials:** Charcoal, salt, laundry bluing, small glass bowl.

In the evening before the child goes to bed, put a few lumps of charcoal in a shallow glass bowl. Add 2 tablespoons each of water, bluing and salt. The next morning there will be beautiful, coral-like crystals on the charcoal.

You can also add a few drops of food coloring for more colorful crystals.

---

**Helpful hint:** Crystals grow best on charcoal. If you don't have charcoal, a tablespoon of ammonia added to the mixture will produce crystals on a sponge or other porous material.

---

Would your grandchild like to make something with this crystal garden? Here's an idea:

## Crystals and fish

**Materials:** Things used to grow crystals, a small fish bowl, colored construction paper, markers, needle and thread.

❑ Grow crystals in a small fish bowl.
❑ Cut fish shapes from colored construction paper.
❑ With marker, add eyes, fins and scales.

❑ Poke a tiny hole in each fish near its center of gravity. Use needle and thread to suspend fish from a support placed across the top of the fish bowl.

Fish will appear to swim in a coral decorated fish bowl.

## Candy crystals

These crystals grow slowly and are not as spectacular.
**Materials:** Sugar, water, string, drinking glass.

You (the grandparent) boil 2 cups of sugar and one cup of water in a saucepan. Cool 15 minutes and add another cup of sugar. Stir until the sugar dissolves. Place a string in the sugar water. Wait a few days for crystals to form on the string.

## Grow a plant

Ask your grandchild if he or she thinks a bean will grow into a plant. If you have nasturtium seeds, you can ask the child if he or she would like to grow a plant to take home – a present for Mommy. Nasturtiums grow quickly and do not require special soil, in fact, they seem to do best in sandy soil.

**Materials:** Plastic or Styrofoam drinking cups, water glass, clean dirt from the back yard, gravel, a few dry beans, paper towels.

**Optional Materials:** Potting soil, Pearlite, a few kernels of popcorn, a few grains of rice, packet of nasturtium seeds.

❑ Scoop clean dirt into a pan or buy a bag of potting soil.

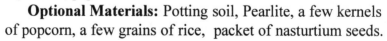

❑ Punch a small hole in the bottom of several plastic drinking cups.

❑ Place gravel (or if you do a lot of potting you might use Pearlite) in the bottom of the cup. This provides drainage and won't clog the hole in the bottom of the cup.

❑ Put dirt or potting soil on top of gravel. Fill the cup.

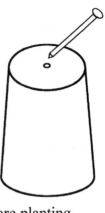

❑ Pour in water. Soil should be damp before planting seeds.

❑ Grandchild can make a hole for the seed by sticking his or her finger into the soil up to the first joint.

❑ Drop a seed into this hole, cover with soil.

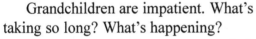

❑ Wait, water and watch.

Grandchildren are impatient. What's taking so long? What's happening?

You can provide the answers to their questions. Put crushed paper towel in a drinking glass.

Place a bean with a piece of folded towel behind it against the glass. Wet the paper towel and watch what happens.

Keep water in the glass, but not too much. Too much water causes the bean to rot, instead of grow.

Now your grandchild can see the root form, watch the bean split, push upward and become seed-leaves.

## Grow a pinecone garden

**Materials:** Large pine cone, grass seed, saucer of water.

Set pine cone in a saucer of water. Plant grass between the pine cone's sections. Water each day and wait for grass to grow.

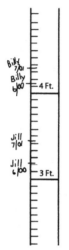

## Make a height chart

And while we're on the subject of the miracle of growth, how about making a height chart?

Tape or tack a large sheet of butcher paper to the wall. Each year when the grandchild comes for a visit, mark a line on the paper to show his or her height and write the child's name and the date on the paper.

## Make a life-size body

Instead of measuring your grandchild's height on a wall chart, make a life-size drawing.

**Material:** 5 ft. of butcher paper, pencil, crayons or poster paint.

Put butcher paper on the floor and have your grandchild lie down on it. Trace around the child's body.

Let your grandchild draw in the face, clothing and shoes. Color, cut out and hang on the wall.

Be sure to write the child's name and age on the back of the life-size figure.

## Record fun memories

Take pictures. Use a camcorder or camera to record and save the joys of your grandchild's visit.

You could make a scrapbook for each of your grandchildren. When they visit, write the date at the top of a new page, add a few pictures, mementoes and the child's hand written story of an interesting part of the vacation.

Suggestions for mementoes:

❑ Ticket stubs from places you visited.

❑ Autographs from famous or interesting people you met.

❑ A dried, pressed flower from a favorite picnic spot.

## IN THE BACK-YARD

### Build a tree house

This project is a sure-fire winner and will provide your grandchildren with many hours of fun.

**Materials:** A tree in the backyard, lumber, nails, hammer, saw.

Grandpa should build a sturdy platform in the tree with a strong rail around the outer edge. This will prevent the young builder from falling.

After the platform is securely anchored in place, turn the building over to the grandchild. He or she will scrounge pieces of old lumber, pasteboard boxes and paint.

The tree house will be unique and probably never quite finished. One day it will be a clubhouse attracting kids from around the neighborhood and the next day it will be the

crow's nest in an old time sailing ship and the children will be
pirates.

---

**Helpful hint:** Do not make the
tree house too high. Eight feet off
the ground will seem as tall as the
Eiffel Tower to a ten-year-old. The
smaller the child, the lower the
platform should be.

---

### Plant a garden

Make a plan. Discuss what you are going to plant.
Then with Grandma and Grandpa's help, spade up the dirt,
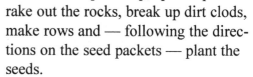 rake out the rocks, break up dirt clods,
make rows and — following the direc-
tions on the seed packets — plant the
seeds.

Water, watch, wait and weed.

After the grandchild goes home, the
garden will be your responsibility.

Take pictures and send garden
reports (by letter, e-mail or telephone) to
your grandchild. Maybe Thanksgiving
dinner could include pumpkin pies made
from pumpkins grown in your grandchild's garden.

### Jump rope

Introduce your grandchild to old-fashioned jump rope –
two people turn the rope and one person jumps.

**Material:** Rope approximately 3/8 inch in diameter and at
least 10 feet long.

I have reached the age when I would rather turn the rope
than jump. But that's okay, because grandkids would rather
jump than turn.

Teach your grandchild some old-fashioned jump rope rhymes. Remember this one?

*Mable, Mable set the table.*
*Don't forget to skim the milk. (Turners raise the rope*
*off the ground while turning.)*
*Mable, Mable set the table.*
*Don't forget the salt, vinegar, pepper. (Turners turn*
*the rope faster and faster on the words, "salt, vinegar,*
*pepper.")*

### Chinese jump rope

**Material:** One Chinese jump rope (costs about a dollar at most variety stores.)
**Number of Players:** Three.

Two people stand about 3 ft. apart with Chinese jump rope (6 ft. elastic band) looped around their ankles and stretched between them.

The jumper hooks the front rope over one foot and hops over the back rope. Then he or she hops backward to original position without touching the back rope.

Other more difficult maneuvers are diagramed on the card that comes with the Chinese jump rope.

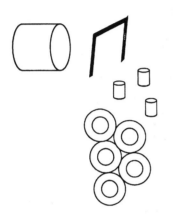

### Run an obstacle course

It's as much fun to make as it is to run through it.

**Materials:** Things found in the back yard, empty milk cartons or tin cans (no sharp edges).

Look for things to run through or jump over. Old tires (you must step inside each tire when running the course), empty milk cartons or tin cans to mark turns, and things to climb over or crawl under. After helping construct the obstacle course out of whatever you happen to have, you become the timekeeper. Use a watch with a second hand to measure the child's time.

### Blow bubbles

**Materials:** Concentrated liquid dishwashing detergent, glycerin, bendable wire.

#### Bubble recipe:
*1 cup liquid detergent*
*4 cups water*
*1 teaspoon glycerin*

❑ Put the bubble mixture in a large shallow pan.

❑ Twist wire into a bubble wand.

❑ Blow bubbles.

Any object that has a loop can become a wand. Experiment! Old glasses frames make double-bubble blowers. Try blowing bubbles with wire mesh.

> **Helpful hint**: Do this on a hot summer day. It's a wet, messy activity. But getting wet is all part of the fun.

For a very young grandchild, buy a bottle of bubble mix. Cost is less than 50 cents and available in any toy department.

Keep it handy for major crises, such as a skinned knee. You can whip out the bubble mix and change tears to smiles. Well – it sometimes works!

## Fun with balloons

Two and three-year-olds love balloons, especially helium-filled ones.

Air-filled balloons can also amuse a small child. With colored marker, draw a happy face on a balloon.

Let your toddler bounce Mr. Happy Face on the end of a string. Or let the air swoosh out of Mr. Happy Face sending him swirling around like an out-of-control rocket.

Older grandchildren also love balloons, especially water filled ones.

## Throw water balloons

Throwing water balloons is very much like throwing snowballs. On a hot summer day, make a few ground rules, such as, no throwing at your opponent's face or head, and let the battle begin. Most grandparents would rather be spectators than participants in this game and that's okay because a referee (someone to call time out) is often needed.

## Water balloon toss

Grandma can play this game. The game starts with two people standing about three feet apart. A water balloon is tossed back and forth. Each time the balloon is caught the player takes a step backward.

Greater distance requires harder throws. Eventually the balloon breaks. *Splash!*

# IN THE NEIGHBORHOOD

## Go for a walk

You walk and talk. This is one of the times when real grandparent-grandchild bonding occurs.

## Go for a drive

For Grandparents who find walking difficult, going for a drive together accomplishes the same purpose.

Several times I've been asked to pick up Kevin after school and give him a ride home or to our house. If you are ever asked to give a grandchild a ride home after school, do it.

The smile you get when the child sees Grandma is there to meet him is priceless.

## Ride bicycles

Do you have a bicycle and enjoy riding? If you do, then ask your grandchild to bring a bicycle to your house. Or you might rent a bicycle or buy one at a yard sale.

## Make a lemonade stand

**Materials:** Large box or table, large sheet of construction paper or butcher paper, poster paint, masking tape.

The most important part of the lemonade stand is the sign to attract customers. On a large sheet of paper, paint "LEMONADE" and also the price per glass. Tape the sign on the front of the stand (a box or table).

Location is second most important. If your house is on a busy street, the sidewalk in front of your home will do nicely. If not, ask friends who live in a better location to let you and your grandchildren set up business in front of their home.

## How to make lemonade

**Materials:** Frozen lemonade concentrate, ice, pitcher, paper cups.

Mix lemonade in a pitcher according to the directions on the can. Supply the entrepreneurs with ice, pitcher, paper cups and money for making change (a loan which must be repaid).

After the stand is set up, buy a glass of lemonade and relax on a lounge chair nearby with a book while the children wait on customers.

## Go to the park or playground

Walk or ride to the neighborhood playground. Once there all you have to do is watch or maybe push a swing.

Or you could:

### Fly a kite

**Material**: Kite (the simple inexpensive kind, like the one you had when you were a child, or an expensive stunt kite), a ball of string or twine.

On a breezy day take your grandchild and a kite to a park or vacant lot. Grandma and Grandpa can join in the fun with kites, too. Stunt kites increase the fun, but they are expensive.

### Throw a boomerang

**Material:** Twelve-inch square of heavy cardboard.
**Optional material:** Water-soluble paint.

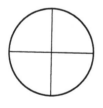

❑ Set a large round plate on cardboard cut from the side of a box and trace around it.

❑ Draw a line across the circle from top to bottom and side to side. (The circle should look like a pie marked into 4 equal pieces.)

❑ From a point where the line touches the edge of the circle, draw a curve (like the beginning of an S) toward the center; stop when the curve reaches a point about halfway to the center. Repeat at each intersection of line and circle.

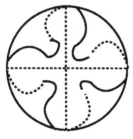

❑ Draw a curved line in the opposite direction from the point where the line touches the edge of the circle. Connect this curved line to the curved line from the corner to the right. Repeat at each corner.

❑ Does your figure look like the blades of a fan? If not, redraw the lines. When you have the shape you want, cut it out. You can paint it or leave it plain.

## Boomerang fun

On a relatively clam day, throw the boomerang like a Frisbee into the breeze. The boomerang will spin up and up, reach its highest point and spin down, down back to you or close to you. It may take a little practice.

## Play catch with a Frisbee

If you don't want to make a boomerang, you can always have fun at the park playing catch with a Frisbee.

## Feed ducks or fish

Is there a duck or fish pond in your neighborhood park? Take a sack of stale bread or popcorn to the park and feed the ducks or fish.

## Special neighborhood attractions

Here are some fun places to go with grandkids. Depending on what's in your area, you could:

## Go to the zoo

Kids love animals. You don't have to see everything, but don't miss the monkeys.

## Go to a children's museum

Adult museums are boring, but more and more museums

have interactive displays that make a trip to the museum fun.

### Visit the library

Let your grandchild pick a favorite book to be read at bedtime.

### See a movie

Is the latest release for kids playing at your local theater?

### Splash at a water park

Great fun for kids.  Not so much fun for Grandma and Grandpa.

### Visit an amusement park

If you live close to a major amusement park this could be the highlight of the visit.

### Go fishing

Some grandchildren like to go fishing; others find the inactivity boring.

---

**Warning:** If fishing involves going out in a boat, everyone should wear a PFD (Personal Floatation Device) – Grandma and Grandpa, as well as the kids.

---

## Go swimming

Whether swimming or wading this activity is usually a big hit with grandkids, but should be closely supervised. And while floating toys add to the fun, they also add to the danger.

> **Warning:** Do not let young children or non-swimmers play on inner tubes or floating toys. These toys pose a real danger. Wind can push a floatation toy out into deep water faster than a strong swimmer can swim. **Never swim after or allow a child to swim after a wind-blown floating toy.**

## Enjoy a picnic

Kids love a picnic and part of the fun is planning and helping Grandma prepare the food. A picnic can be combined with almost any of the *In the Neighborhood* activities, as well as be a part of your next road trip.

## On the road

Maybe you've planned a trip as part of your summer fun, or maybe it's a cross-country trek by automobile to bring the grandchildren to your house or take them home.

In any event, when children are cooped up for long periods of time in a car, there will be problems. Kids need something to do. If they can't get exercise any other way, they will bounce around and kick the back of your seat.

Suggestions:

❑ Buy *Kid's Travel Fun Book* by Loris & Marlin Bree. This little book is full of practical ideas for amusing youngsters on a long trip.

❑ Stop often. Run races. Get out the Frisbee and play catch. Do anything that will use some of the grandchild's pent up energy.

❑ Pack a picnic lunch and eat at a roadside rest stop. This will save money, save time and save wear and tear on your nerves.

## WHEN THINGS GO WRONG

Doing things with your grandchild is what grandparent-grandchild bonding is all about.

But…

Suppose you've made plans, provided games, suggested activities with great enthusiasm and praised your grandchild's ideas; and still the child is bored, cranky and unhappy. **Don't blame yourself, and don't blame the kid.** Maybe your grandchild is too young to be away from home. Maybe the child has problems which inhibit his or her ability to interact with others.

If you're not having fun and the grandchild is not having fun, take him or her home and try again next year. Remind yourself that you do not have to raise this child – that's the parent's responsibility.

Several years ago, Dr. Theresa Smith, director of Lake Mead Academy (a school in Boulder City, Nevada, for children with special problems) gave me this advice about grandchildren:

"You don't have to teach these grandkids. You don't have to bring them up. You don't have to give them all the moral values. You just *enjoy* them."

# 5

# Let's make something!

## GIFTS

### Small vase or pencil holder

**Materials:** A small glass jar, tissue paper in a variety of colors, non-toxic glue.

❑ Wash and dry a small glass jar.

❑ Cut tissue paper into small squares (about 1 inch square).

❑ Using glue thinned with a little water, paste the tissue paper pieces on the jar. Overlap. Randomly select colors.

❑ After the jar is entirely covered, paste a long narrow strip of tissue paper around the top to make a finished edge.

❑ As a final touch you might add a few hearts or flower shapes or even a few sequins.

❑ When the glue is dry paint the jar with a thin coat of glue mixed with water.

And there you have it, a perfect take-home gift for Mommy or Daddy.

### Potholders

**Materials:** Cotton cloth, felt, needle, embroidery thread.

❑ Draw a pattern for the shape you want on a piece of paper. (Good shapes are squares, circles, or a simple object such as a teapot.)

❑ Pin the pattern on the cloth and cut out. Cut two cloth shapes and one felt lining.

❑ Trim the felt lining, make it a little smaller than cloth pieces.

❑ Make a sandwich with cloth, lining and cloth. Pin the three pieces together.

❑ Sew together with blanket stitch; use a large needle and embroidery thread.

### Sand bottles

**Materials:** Sand or dirt in various colors, small jars (baby food jars are the right size), sifter or sieve, small funnel, plastic containers (small margarine bowls.)

**Optional material:** Paraffin sealing wax.

❑ Collect various colors of sand or dirt.

❑ Pour dirt through a sifter or sieve to remove large particles and collect it in small plastic bowls.

Helpful hint: Put a plastic container in the trunk of your car. When you see an unusual color of sand or dirt stop and scoop up some.

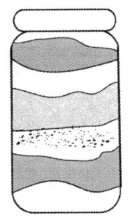

❑ Keep each color in a separate container.

❑ After sifting the sand pour it in layers into a clean jar. Use a small funnel or paper cone with tip removed to pile the sand high in some places.

❑ Alternate light and dark colors.

❑ Sand bottles can be used for paperweights or simply as decorations.

❑ After filling the bottle, Grandma could pour a quarter inch of paraffin over the sand. (Sealing is optional.) When the wax hardens it will hold the sand in place.

**Warning:** Hot paraffin can cause sever burns and is flammable. **Do not let a child heat or pour wax.**

## Bookmark

**Materials:** Construction paper, crayons or colored pencils or water-soluble markers.

Cut a strip of construction paper in a width and length suitable for a bookmark (approximately 2¼" wide and 7½" long) and decorate. Or add a pressed flower.

**Pressed flowers**

**Materials:** Flower, blotting paper, newspapers, a heavy book.

❑ Put newspaper on a flat surface. Lay blotting paper on top of the newspaper.

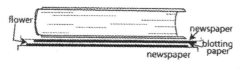

❑ Carefully arrange flower on the blotting paper and cover with a second sheet of blotting paper and more newspaper.

❑ Place something heavy such as a board and a heavy book on top.

❑ Wait one week.

❑ Glue the pressed flower on the bookmark with a spot of glue and let it dry. Cover with Contact paper or laminate.

> **Helpful hint:** Positioning and pulling the backing off the Contact paper is a job for Grandma. It must be done right the first time – no second chances.

## Quick and easy pressed flowers

Here's a faster, easier way to make a pressed flower bookmark:

❑ Gather a few flowers, such as daisies, from Grandparent's garden. Pull flower petals off the blossom and a few leaves off the stem.

❑ Cut thin cardboard about 2 inches wide and 7 inches long.

❑ Cover the bookmark with a thin coat of glue.

❑ Arrange petals in a flower shape. Add a few green leaves.

❑ Let glue dry. Press over night between the pages of a book. (Because this bookmark is made with only thin petals and leaves, the flower shape dries quickly.)

❑ Laminate or cover with clear contact paper.

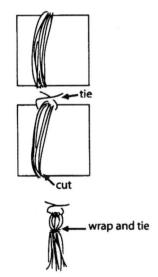

## Bookmark tassel

**Materials:** Yarn, 3-inch square of cardboard.

❑ Wrap yarn around cardboard square.

❑ Slide a piece of yarn under the wrapped yarn and tie at the top of the card.

❑ Cut wrapped yarn at the bottom of the card.

❑ Wrap another piece of yarn around the tassel and tie. (See diagram.)

## Plaster of Paris jewelry

**Materials:** Plaster of Paris, string or yarn, water-soluble paint, disposable container, waxed paper.

❑ Mix Plaster of Paris with water in a disposable container. (The bottom half of a half-gallon cardboard milk carton works well.)

❑ Place string or yarn on waxed paper.

❑ Drop Plaster of Paris globs one inch apart on the string or yarn.

❑ Wait two or three hours till globs dry, then paint with water-soluble paint.

❑ Long strings make necklaces. Short strings make bracelets.

## Paper beads

**Materials:** White typing paper or colored construction paper, non-toxic glue.

**Optional material:** Water soluble paint.

❑ Cut paper in long thin strips – about a ½ inch wide and 10 to 12 inches long.

❑ Taper. (Cut away both

sides of strip to form a long slender point.)

❑ Start at wide end and roll paper like a tight jellyroll.

❑ Spread glue on the last inch of the roll.

❑ Hold the bead between thumb and finger for a few seconds while glue dries.

❑ If white paper is used, the beads can be painted with water-soluble paint.

### Play clay beads

**Materials**: Commercial or home-made play clay, straws, water colors, brushes.

Shape your favorite play clay around a thin straw in artful shapes. Dry at lowest heat in the oven and paint with water-soluble paint.

### Pasta beads

**Materials:** Pasta with holes, water-soluble poster paint.

❑ Paint any kind of pasta that has a hole with poster paint.

❑ Seal with clear nail polish.

### String beads

**Materials:** Paper beads or play dough beads or pasta beads, small wooden beads, yarn or string, needle with a large eye.

Making beads is tedious work. Your grandchild may soon tire of this activity. This is when you bring out the wooden beads and let him or her start making a necklace.

Thread a large-eye needle with yarn or string. Use both wooden beads and handmade beads to make a bracelet or necklace.

## Plaster of Paris hand plaque

**Materials:** Plaster of Paris, pie plate or paper plate, disposable container.

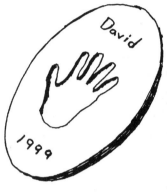

❑ Mix Plaster of Paris in disposable container.

❑ Pour plaster into a greased pie tin or sturdy paper plate and let it partially harden.

❑ Place the child's hand in the center of the plate with fingers spread and push down. Grandparent should press each finger firmly into the plaster.

❑ Lift and wash the child's hand.

❑ Wait two or three hours and carefully slide the hand plaque out of the pan.

❑ Write the date and the child's name on the back.

❑ You may want to make two hand plaques – one for the child to take home and one for Grandma and Grandpa to keep.

## Refrigerator magnet

**Materials:** Play clay, water-soluble paint, clear nail polish or shellac, magnetic tape.

❑ Shape play dough into small flat objects (such as, fish, hearts, letters).

❑ Put play dough in the oven on a cookie sheet.

❑ Set oven at lowest temperature setting and allow play dough to harden.

❑ Paint the shape and cover with clear nail polish or shellac.

❑ Glue magnetic tape on the back.

> **Helpful hint:** This is a messy activity. Dye has a way of getting on everything and everybody. It is best to do this in the back yard and wear old clothes.

## Tie-dye T-shirt

Tie-dye T-shirts could be uniforms for your grandchild and neighborhood kids (members of a club).

**Material:** Clean white T-shirt, commercial dye, large rubber bands or string, large pan for dying, washing machine.

❑ Prepare dye according to package directions.

❑ Bunch T-shirt material and secure with rubber bands or tie with string. Make several ties.

❑ Dip in dye until color is slightly darker than desired.

❑ After dying the shirt, rinse it in cold water to which a small amount of salt has been added.

❑ Machine wash separately in cold water.

❑ Remove rubber bands and dry.

## Decorated wrapping paper

Wrap the take-home gift in handmade wrapping paper. The paper will be treasured as well as the gift.

**Materials:** Paper (tissue paper, newsprint or brown paper bags), acrylic or tempera paint, vegetables (such as green peppers, carrots, potatoes).

❑ Pour paint into a saucer.
❑ Cut vegetables in half (crosswise or longwise).
❑ Dip vegetable in paint and print on tissue paper. (You can make many prints with just one dip.)
❑ Allow paint to dry before wrapping gift.

## Flowers on wrapping paper

**Materials:** Paper, paintbrush, tempera paint, watercolors.

❑ Dip brush in white tempera then roll brush in a bright color of watercolor – red, yellow or orange.
❑ Print (don't paint) the petals of the flower with the flat side of the brush.
Your grandchild will be pleased to see how easy it is to make beautiful flowers.

## TOYS

## Milk carton boat

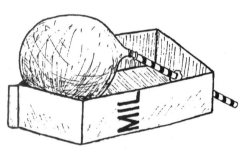

**Materials:** Half-gallon milk carton, sturdy plastic drinking straw, round balloon, rubber band, modeling clay.

❑ Cut away the spout and side of a milk carton.
❑ Make a small hole in the bottom of the opposite side.
❑ Reinforce the plastic straw. Cut straw in half. Crimp the end of one half and insert it into the other half. This makes a double thick straw.
❑ Fasten the balloon to the drinking straw with rubber band.

❑ Put the straw through the hole in the bottom of the milk carton and seal the hole around the straw with a little bit of modeling clay.

❑ Inflate the balloon by blowing through the straw. Hold your finger over the end of the straw or pinch shut to keep air in the balloon.

❑ Put boat in the water.

Your jet-propelled craft is ready for a race!

### Styrofoam or wood block boat

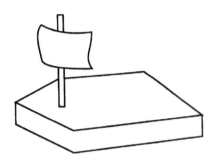

**Materials:** Pieces of Styrofoam or chunks of wood, glue, serrated knife or handsaw.

Give your creative grandchild pieces of Styrofoam packing, such as you might find in the box that a new appliance came in, or use chunks of wood from a carpenter's workshop. With minimal guidance from a grandparent, let the child design and create his own unique boat.

**Warning:** Grandparent should operate the serrated knife or saw.

### Paper boats

Paper boats are easy to make but are generally very unstable. The exception is one found in **Kid's Travel Fun Book** by Lois & Marlin Bree.

This sailboat will actually float! With a bathtub of water and a big wind supplied by huffing and puffing grandparents and grandkids, you can have sailboat races.

# How to make a paper boat
# that floats and sails

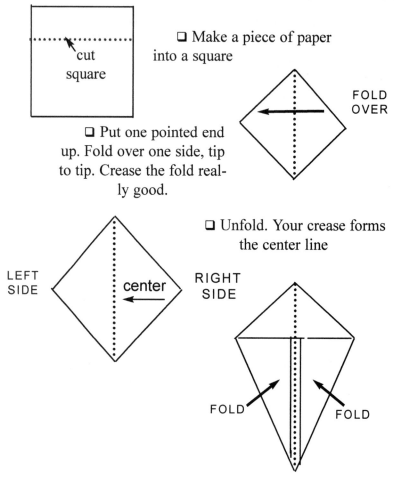

❑ Make a piece of paper into a square

cut square

FOLD OVER

❑ Put one pointed end up. Fold over one side, tip to tip. Crease the fold really good.

❑ Unfold. Your crease forms the center line

LEFT SIDE

center

RIGHT SIDE

FOLD

FOLD

❑ Fold the right side to the center line. Then fold the left side to the center line, as shown.

Paper boat illustrations and text are from *Kid's Travel Fun Book,* published by Marlor Press, used with permission of the authors.

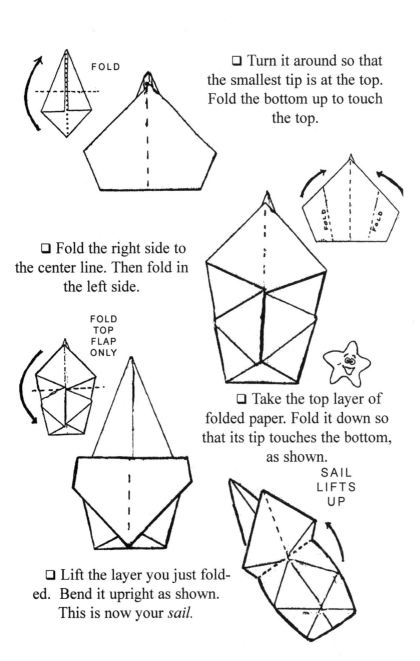

FOLD

❑ Turn it around so that the smallest tip is at the top. Fold the bottom up to touch the top.

❑ Fold the right side to the center line. Then fold in the left side.

FOLD
FOLD

FOLD
TOP
FLAP
ONLY

❑ Take the top layer of folded paper. Fold it down so that its tip touches the bottom, as shown.

SAIL
LIFTS
UP

❑ Lift the layer you just folded. Bend it upright as shown. This is now your *sail*.

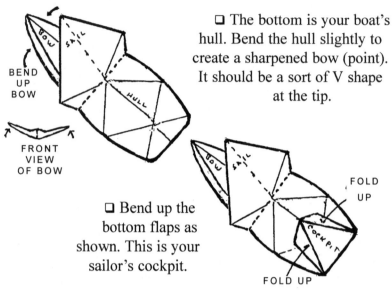

□ The bottom is your boat's hull. Bend the hull slightly to create a sharpened bow (point). It should be a sort of V shape at the tip.

□ Bend up the bottom flaps as shown. This is your sailor's cockpit.

□ Give your little boat a name and decorate it. You can color the sail.

□ Put your boat in some water (a bathtub will do) and blow on the sail from behind. Watch it go!

**IDEAS:** You can make a several little racers to hold sailboat races. These paper boats will last in the water for a number of races before they get waterlogged (depending on the paper you use). We used ordinary computer printer paper, but any type of paper that will hold a fold will do, including heavy wrapping paper. When your boat gets too wet to sail, you can let it dry out to sail later. And you can easily make some more. *Fun!*

## Flying a paper airplane

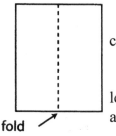

fold

**Materials:** One sheet typing paper, paper clip.

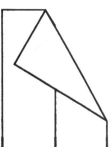

❑ Fold paper in half lengthwise. Make a crease and then open and lay flat.

❑ Fold right corner up and slightly over middle fold. Crease, then open and lay flat.

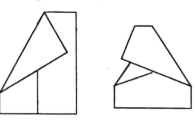

❑ Fold left corner up and refold right corner over top of left side.

❑ Turn the plane over and fold down left-over flap.

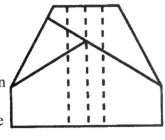

❑ Fold about 3 inches of nose back over airplane and refold and crease nose and entire airplane on center line.

❑ Turn over (folded-back nose is now on bottom) and fold the right wing down about an inch from fold.

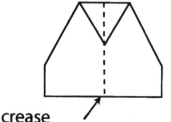

crease

❑ Fold the left wing down about an inch from the center fold. (There are now several thicknesses of paper in the nose so press and crease firmly.)

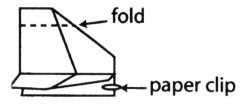

fold

paper clip

❑ Fasten the two sides of the nose together with a paper clip.

Your plane is now ready for a test flight. For greater distance, fold about one inch of wing tip up.

Experiment! Does folding wing tips down improve flight? Try different launching motions, upward or downward.

### Balsa wood airplane

Balsa wood airplane kits are inexpensive, fun to make and available in the toy departments of variety stores.

**Helpful hint:** Buy three kits (one for Grandpa and one for spare parts). These light, high-flying planes have a way of landing on rooftops or crash landing. Avoid tears with an extra airplane kit.

### Plastic-foam airplane

**Material:** Clean plastic-foam meat trays.

Use the pieces of your balsa wood airplane as a pattern and cut an airplane body, wing and tail section from foam meat trays.

Assemble the same way you assembled the balsa wood plane and you are ready for flight.

### Paper hat

**Material:** One sheet of paper approximately 18" by 24" (brown bag or newspaper will do.)

❑ Fold paper in half crosswise and fold in half again.

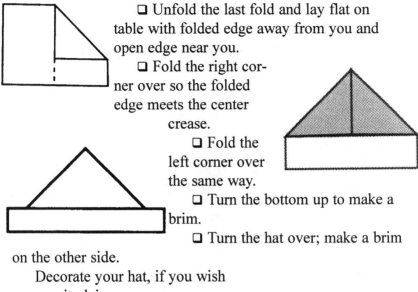

❑ Unfold the last fold and lay flat on table with folded edge away from you and open edge near you.

❑ Fold the right corner over so the folded edge meets the center crease.

❑ Fold the left corner over the same way.

❑ Turn the bottom up to make a brim.

❑ Turn the hat over; make a brim on the other side.

Decorate your hat, if you wish or wear it plain.

## How to make a top

**Materials:** 8 or 10 dessert-size paper plates, pencil, 2 sewing thread spools, rubber bands, paint, sequins, glitter.

❑ Find the center of one paper plate by balancing the plate on the eraser end of your pencil.

❑ With a sharp pointed scissors or nail punch a hole in the plate. (This is a job for grandparent.) Use the hole in the first plate to mark and punch the center hole on the other plates.

❑ Push a pencil through one thread spool, the paper plates and the second spool. Spools and plates should fit tightly on the pencil.

❑ Use rubber bands to hold spools and plates securely in place.

❑ Decorate and spin.

Launch top by holding the pencil between palms. Quickly

move one hand forward, the other hand backward and drop top. Your grandkid will show you how to do it.

As the top spins the design and colors you used to decorate it will blend making new colors and patterns.

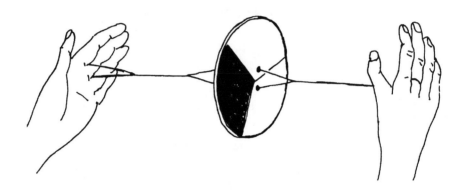

## Magic-spin
## color wheel

**Material:** Red, yellow and blue paper, a large button or cardboard circle, glue, string.

❑ Glue red, yellow and blue paper on both sides of a large button or a cardboard circle cut 2½ inches in diameter. (A large button is easier to use and gives better results.)

❑ Thread a four-foot string through the two holes in the button. (If you use cardboard you will need to make two holes ¼ inch from center.)

❑ Tie the ends of the string so that it makes a continuous loop.

❑ Twist the loop, place the ends over the index finger of each hand, and then alternately tauten and loosen the string.

❑ The wheel spins and the colors mix to form new colors.

## Make a pinwheel

**Materials:** Construction paper, corsage pin, glue, unsharpened pencil with eraser, small plastic or wooden bead.

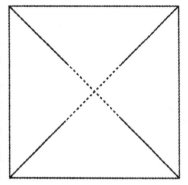

❑ Cut construction paper into an 8-inch square.

❑ Place a ruler from corner to corner. (See diagram.)

❑ Mark and cut a little more than halfway to the center.

❑ Bend right-hand tips into the center. (Do not fold.) Secure in the center with a small drop of glue.

❑ Put pin through the center of the pinwheel, the bead and into the side of the pencil eraser.

The pinwheel will spin as you move it.

### Paper bag flashlight faces

After a day filled with activities, Grandma, Grandpa and Grandchild can unwind with this quite just-before-bedtime activity.

**Materials:** Flash-light, lunch-size paper bags, markers in bold dark colors, rubber bands.

Grandma, Grandpa and Grandchild gather around the kitchen table with paper bags and a handful of markers. Each person makes a funny face on a paper bag.

When finished, it's off to bed where a flashlight is stored under the child's pillow. Secure the paper bag on the flashlight with a rubber band.

Turn on the flashlight to see the face light up.

## Play dough

**Materials:**

| | |
|---|---|
| 1 cup salt | ½ cup cornstarch |
| ¾ cup cold water | acrylic paints or food coloring |

Mix salt, cornstarch and water over low heat. (This is a job for Grandma.) Stir constantly. When mixture thickens turn out on waxed paper and cool. Knead to improve texture.

With this dough the child can make animal shapes or roll between hands to make a long rope which can then be used to form letters. When the child has the shape he or she wants, the clay can be dried in an oven set at a very low temperature.

## Crazy clay

Kids love the feel of this dough that strings, stretches and molds but will not hold its shape. Grandparents love it because it forms a pliable ball, adheres to itself and is not messy.

One exception: when allowed to soak into fabric it is difficult to get out. Therefore, when the child is not playing with this clay, keep it in a plastic bag.

**Materials:**

½ cup white glue      ¼ cup liquid starch

Mix glue and starch together. Moisten hands with liquid starch and work the dough into a smooth ball. If the ball begins to stick to your grandchild's hands, you can moisten his or her hands with more starch.

Two and three-year-olds will play with this clay for hours. They stretch out long thin strings or roll it into a ball – a ball that bounces. After you're done, wash hands carefully.

## How to make a play clay

**Materials:**

3 cups flour              1 cup salt
½ cup vegetable oil    1 cup water

❑ Make a hole in the flour and salt mixture and add a little oil and a little water. Stir until smooth.

❑ Add more water and oil a little at a time.

❑ Stir flour mixture into the liquid until it makes a smooth paste.

❑ Food coloring can be added for colored clay.

❑ Knead mixture on waxed paper. If too dry, add water by wetting hands before kneading.

The advantage of this clay over regular play dough is that it does not dry out. It can be used over and over and then put in a plastic bag and stored for use at a later time.

You and your grandchild might use this clay to make a volcano.

## How to make
## a volcano that erupts

**Materials:** Clay or mud, small glass (such as the kind cheese spreads come in) baking soda, water, detergent, vinegar, food coloring.

❑ Mold clay or mud in the shape of a volcano around a small slender glass.

❑ Twigs may be stuck into the mud or clay near the base of the volcano to simulate trees.

❑ Put 3 teaspoons of baking soda in the glass.

❑ Mix together: ¼ cup water, 2 tablespoons detergent, 3 tablespoons vinegar, a drop of red food coloring.

❑ Pour this mixture into glass.

❑ Volcano will erupt!

> **Helpful hint:** Do this in the back yard or, if inside the house, build the volcano on a large dinner plate and spread newspapers under the plate. Your grandchild will love to see the "red lava" cascading down the sides of the volcano, but unless you are prepared for the mess, you will not be so delighted.

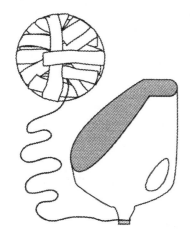

## Toss and catch game

**Materials:** Newspaper, duct tape or masking tape, string, half-gallon plastic milk bottle with handle.

❑ Crush newspapers to make a ball. (The ball must be small enough to easily slip inside the cut-off milk bottle.)

❑ Tape a three-foot long string to the ball. Use lots of tape. This will hold the newspaper in a ball shape and also hold string in place.

❑ Cut a plastic milk bottle in half. Tie the end of the string to the handle of the milk bottle.

Now you and your grandchild are ready to play the game. Place the newspaper ball in the milk bottle. Toss it in the air and try to catch it in the milk bottle.

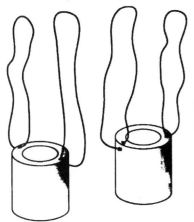

## How to make old-fashioned stilts

**Materials:** Empty milk cans, heavy string or twine, ice pick or drill.

❑ Punch or drill holes on opposite sides of two empty milk cans. (This is a job for a grandparent.)

❑ Thread string or twine through the holes.

❑ Tie ends of strings to make long loops. Loops should be long enough to reach from the tops of the milk cans to the child's hands when he or she is standing on the cans.

The child walks on the cans while pulling on the string loops to hold the cans against his or her feet.

## Taller stilts

An older child (ten years or older) might want taller stilts. The adult should be in charge of this project — nailing and testing stilts for strength.

Grandkid can be a helper – measuring, holding boards and smoothing the handle with a plane.

**Materials:** Two boards (approximately 1¼" by 1¼"), saw, hammer, large nails or large screws, plane or lathe, metal corner brackets.

❑ Cut the two boards. The length of each board should be equal to the height of the grandkid.

❑ Nail or screw 4-inch blocks of wood no more than 8 inches from the bottom of the stilt. (Eight inches off the ground is plenty high for a first-time stilt-walker.)

❑ Reinforce with metal corner brackets. (See diagram.)

❑ Use plane or lathe to smooth and round the tops of the stilts to make handles.

**Warning**: Stilts must be strong enough to hold twice the child's weight. A broken stilt can cause a bad fall or serious injury.

---

**Helpful hint:** An old vinyl
tablecloth or a shower curtain used
to cover the work area makes for
quick easy clean-up.

---

## DECORATIONS

Before your grandchild arrives, collect a box of materials
that could be used for decorating.

Save such things as: scraps of cloth, ribbons, lace, sequins,
yarn and extra buttons. Ask at a wallpaper store if you could
have one of their discarded wallpaper books. Save your old
Christmas cards – they often contain pictures and foil which
can be cut out and reused.

Spread your collection of decorating materials, plus glue
and paint, out on a newspaper-covered work area and let your
grandchild's creative genius take over.
You will be surprised! Ordinary
objects become "works of art."

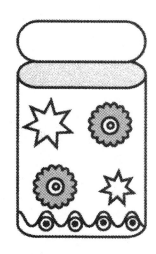

### Decorated crayon box

**Materials:** Metal first-aid box
(such as the ones tapes come in),
water-soluble paint, stickers or pictures cut from magazines, clear shellac, glue.

**Optional materials:** Sequins,
glitter.

---

**Warning:** Shellac is toxic.
Closely supervise its use and store in
a place inaccessible to your
grandchild.

---

❑ Let grandchild choose a color and paint the box. (If paint does not adhere to the metal box add a little liquid detergent to it.)

❑ After the paint dries decorate with whatever materials you have on hand.

❑ Cover the decorated box with clear shellac and your grandchild has a colorful place to store his or her crayons.

If your grandchild enjoyed decorating a first-aid box, look around your house for other ordinary things to decorate:

❑ Empty coffee cans make good flower pots or vases.

❑ Old cigar boxes can become jewelry boxes.

❑ Paper plates can easily turn into wall plaques.

Cover the work area with newspapers, spread out the decorating materials and let your young crafter create. Your job is to encourage, suggest, prevent mishaps (like spilled paint), clean up messes and — above all praise results.

If your grandchild wants or needs a directed activity you might show him or her how to make a paper-plate wall plaque or letter holder.

### Paper plate plaque

**Materials:** Paper plate, small shell macaroni, glue, string, tempera paint or spray paint, plastic or silk flowers.

❑ Make two small holes in the plate.

❑ Thread string through the holes and tie, making a loop for hanging the wall plaque.

❑ Glue shell macaroni around the edge of the plate.

❑ Paint with tempera or spray paint.

❑ Cover the unsightly holes you made in the plate for string loop by gluing plastic or silk flowers over the holes.

❑ A second paper plate cut in half and glued to the front of the first plate turns a wall plaque into a letter holder (a place to stash bills that come in the mail).

**Warning:** Spray painting should be closely supervised – both for the child's safety and the safety of objects that might be damaged by the over-spray.

## Rock or seashell creatures

A rock or a seashell can become (with paint and glue) a mouse, a duck or almost anything.

**Materials:** Small rocks with unusual shapes or various sizes of seashells, glue, water-soluble paint, stick-on eyes (you can buy them in any craft store) clear shellac.

Cover your work area with plenty of newspapers, spread out the materials and let your grandchild's creativity take over.

Kids have terrific imaginations. Preserve the finished product with a coat of clear shellac. (Remember shellac is toxic.  See above warning.)

Suggestions:

❑ If the finished creations are made of small light weight rocks or seashells, they could be glued to magnetic tape to make unique refrigerator magnets.

❑ Rock creatures make good paperweights – big rocks make doorstops.

❑ Glue a safety pin to a seashell construction and you have a decoration for a dress, coat or jacket.

**Farm diorama**

**Materials:**  Shoebox, construction paper, small one-cup size milk carton.

❑ Place a shoebox on its side. This becomes a miniature stage.

❑ Cover the back of this stage with blue construction paper for sky.

❑ Add brown construction paper mountains.

❑ Cover a one-cup size milk carton with red construction paper to make the barn.

❑ Make fence out of brown construction paper. (See farm activity, Chapter 2)

❑ Add a farmer and animals. These can be pictures cut from magazines, your grandchild's drawings, or miniature animals from a play farm set.

## Marineland diorama

**Materials:** Shoe box, construction paper, thread, clear plastic wrap.

❑ Place shoebox on its side.

❑ Cover the back of the box with blue construction paper for water.

❑ Cut out fish shapes and suspend on threads taped to the top of the diorama.

❑ Spread glue on floor of the diorama and sprinkle with sand. Add a few seashells.

❑ Cover the opening with clear plastic wrap for an underwater effect.

## Doll house

A variation of the diorama is a dollhouse. Use a larger box and cover the back with wallpaper samples. Furnish the house with doll-size furniture. Decorate with materials from grandma's decorating collection.

## A FINAL
## REMINDER

A child's world is often too controlled by adults. Parents, teachers (and even grandparents) tell them what to do and how to do it.

But at Grandma and Grandpa's house, the grandchild's way of making a bookmark, a boat or a diorama is the right way.

When your grandchild makes decisions, the results may not measure up to adult standards of perfection, but **everyone** has fun.

# 6

# Let's celebrate

## SNOW TIME

IF YOU HAVE SNOW in your backyard, that's great! You supply sleds and dishpans for sliding down hills, extra dry socks and mittens to warm cold fingers and toes; and after the snow fun — a warm kitchen and hot chocolate.

However, if you live in a warm, sunny climate, your grandchild can decorate your walls with paper snowflakes and snowmen and you can pretend it's snowing outside.

## Paper snowflakes

**Material:**  White sheets of typing paper.

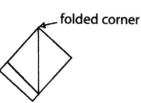

❑ Fold sheet of typing paper in half and then fold in half again.

Lay the paper on a table with folded corner (the corner where all edges are folded) pointing away from you.  Now fold the right side over onto the left side making a point at the top.

Cut off the 1¼ inch of excess paper at the bottom.

Cut wedges and half circles along both sides and across the bottom.  Cut off the point.

Open and you have a snowflake.

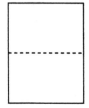

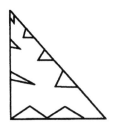

> **Helpful hint**: Be sure when your grandchild folds the right side over onto the left side that the top point has only folded edges. If you don't, your grand-child will end with two sliced-up rectangles instead of one snowflake.

You can tape snowflakes to windows, or decorate refriger-ator and walls.

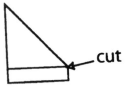

## Paper plate snowman

**Materials:** Regular-size paper plate, dessert-size paper plate, black and red construction paper, glue, string, stapler.

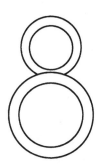

❑ Overlap the dessert plate and dinner plate. Staple them together. Staple a string loop for hanging on the back (concave side) of the dessert plate.

❑ Make patterns on typing paper for top hat, mittens, and mouth.

A penny or dime can serve as a pattern for eyes, nose and buttons.

❑ Lay pattern for hat on black construction paper and trace around it. Cut out hat and glue on the top of the dessert plate.

❑ Make eyes, nose and buttons out of black construction paper. Trace around a penny or dime. Cut out six.

❑ Lay pattern for mouth and mittens on red construction paper. Trace and cut out.

fold under

❑ Place eyes, nose, mouth on the dessert plate and glue in place.

❑ Arrange buttons down the center of the dinner plate and glue in place.

❑ Place mittens on either side of the buttons. Fold the cuff-side of the mittens over the edge of the paper plate and staple in place. Make sure mitten thumbs point up.

## VALENTINE'S DAY

### Valentine hearts

**Material:** Red, pink or white construction paper.

Show your grandchild how to make a heart shape by folding a piece of construction paper and cutting half a heart on the fold.

Now you are ready to make Valentines.

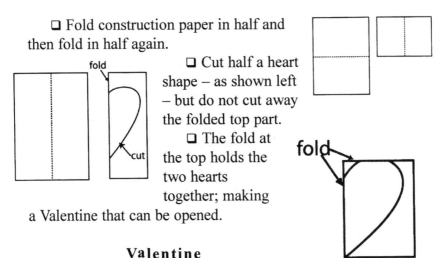

❑ Fold construction paper in half and then fold in half again.

❑ Cut half a heart shape – as shown left – but do not cut away the folded top part.

❑ The fold at the top holds the two hearts together; making a Valentine that can be opened.

## Valentine envelopes

**Materials:** Letter-size envelope (or larger size if your Valentines are larger), wrapping paper, glue.

❑ Open and flatten an envelope that is a size and shape to fit your Valentine and use it as a pattern.

❑ Lay this pattern on wrapping paper or wallpaper.

❑ Trace around it.

❑ Cut along traced lines and using the original envelope as a guide fold and glue the wrapping paper into a new Valentine envelope.

## Old fashioned Valentines

Tell your grandchild about the "good old days" when kids made Valentines out of lace paper doilies, flowers cut from wallpaper books and colored construction paper.

Spread a table or work area with supplies: construction paper, glue, scissors, paper doilies and things from Grandma's decorating collection.

Make Valentines together.

### Valentine keeper

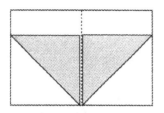

**Materials:** 12" by 18" sheet of red, pink or white construction paper, masking tape, marker, glitter and decorating materials from Grandma's decorating collection.

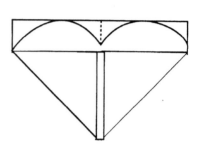

❑ Fold construction paper in half.

❑ Open and fold both corners up and into the center.

❑ Tape center edges together.

❑ With scissors round top corners and make a rounded notch in the center.

❑ Decorate.

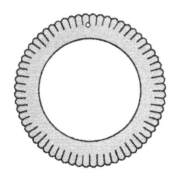

### Valentine wreath

**Materials:** Paper plate, egg carton, paint, glue, string or yarn.

❑ Cut the center out of a paper plate.

❑ Make a hole with a paper punch near the edge and loop string, yarn or ribbon through the hole for hanging.

❑ Paint paper plate green.

❑ Cut egg cups from Styrofoam egg carton for flowers. Cut heart and leaf shapes from the top of the carton.

❑ Paint flowers, hearts and leaves.

❑ Spread glue on the paper plate wreath frame and cover with hearts and flowers.

## Valentine cookies

Make basic sugar cookies. Roll dough out and cut with a heart-shaped cookie cutter. After baking, decorate with butter and powdered sugar frosting. Don't forget to add red food coloring to the frosting. Sprinkle with colored sugars.

## Heart-shaped gelatin jiggle

**Ingredients:** 1½ cup boiling water, 1 large box of strawberry or cherry-flavored gelatin.

❑ Mix boiling water and gelatin. Stir until gelatin completely dissolves. Pour into an eight-inch square pan and chill for three hours.

❑ Loosen gelatin by holding bottom of pan in warm water for 10 seconds. Cut with heart shaped cookie cutter and lift out with spatula.

---

**Warning:** To avoid a bad burn, which could turn fun into disaster, Grandma should heat the water and add it to the gelatin.

---

## Heart refrigerator magnets

**Materials:** Play dough (recipe in Chapter 5) glue, red nail polish, alphabet macaroni, magnetic strip (available in variety and craft stores).

❑ Make small hearts out of play dough and harden in warm (not hot) oven.

❑ Glue magnetic strip on the back of the heart.

❑ Paint with red nail polish.

❑ Write message on heart with alphabet macaroni. (If letters are placed on the heart before the nail polish dries they will stick. Or you can stick them on with glue.)

## EASTER TIME

### Decorating Easter Eggs

**Materials**: Hard-boiled eggs, Easter egg dye, masking tape, glue, things found in Grandma's decorating collection.

### Suggestions:

❑ Follow the directions found on commercial Easter egg dye package. But for variety, try cutting petal and leaf shapes from masking tape. Make a flower design on the egg with tape. Dye the egg. Peel tape off to see the flower pattern.

❑ After dying the eggs a solid color, use things found in Grandma's decorating collection to create faces with hats, bunnies, chicks, lace trimmed fancy eggs or whatever your creative grandchild decides to make.

### Easter egg tree

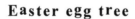

**Materials:**  One dozen eggs, egg dye, glue, stickers, sequins, glitter, thin string or thread,   small bare tree branch, Plaster of Paris, flowerpot or small can.

❑ Dye raw eggs various colors with cold-water dye.
❑ Prick a small hole in both ends of the raw egg. Stick a pin or needle into the egg to break the membrane that surrounds the white and yolk.
❑ Now hold one end of the egg to your mouth and blow.

Blow hard! Keep blowing! The egg comes out – a yellow stringy mess. Expect, "Yucks!" and "Grandma, that's so-o-o gross!"

❑ Now decorate the eggs with stickers, glitter, sequins and things from Grandma's decorating collection.

❑ Mix Plaster of Paris in disposable container. Pour plaster into a flowerpot or small painted can.

❑ After the plaster is partially set, stick a small bare tree branch in center of the flowerpot or can.

❑ Allow plaster to set for three hours.

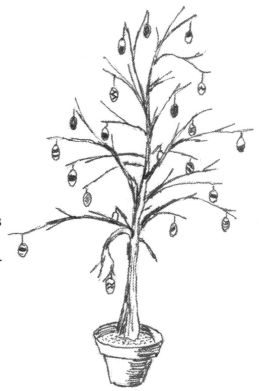

## Make decorated eggs for your Easter Egg Tree

**Materials:** Large wooden or plastic beads, long needle with large eye, string, yarn or crochet cotton.

❑ Thread needle with string, yarn or crochet cotton and tie a bead on the end.

❑ Push needle through the small hole in the bottom of the egg and out through the larger hole at the top.

❑ Add one or two beads at the top.

❑ Tie the string in a loop for hanging and hang eggs on your Easter Tree.

❑ The egg tree will make a lovely centerpiece for your holiday table.

## Make an Easter basket

You can easily make your own Easter basket.

❑ Find a small box and decorate it with things found in Grandma's decorating collection.

❑ Cut a strip of construction paper one inch wide and 12 inches long for a handle. Fold it over for strength.

❑ Staple or glue the handle across the center of the box. This handle is mostly for decoration, not for carrying weight. You can also decorate the handle.

### Easter bonnet

**Materials:** Paper plate, ribbon, water-soluble paint, glue, things found in Grandma's decorating collection.

❑ Spread decorating material out on the kitchen table.

❑ Give grandchild a paper plate with a ribbon threaded through two holes so plate (hat) can be tied on the child's head under the chin.

❑ Give free rein to your child's creative imagination. Glue on items from Grandma's decorating collection, or make your own.

❑ Have an Easter Parade for Grandpa.

## APRIL FOOL FUN

Years ago adults, as well as kids, played April fool jokes. Here's one grownups used to play on each other:

### Bandaged finger

**Materials:** Cork, clean white cloth or gauze.

❑ Wrap cork with white cloth or gauze. Do this by yourself, out of the gaze of your grandchild.

❑ Put a thin strip of cloth around the center of the cork and tie it with the beginning of a simple knot.

❑ Double your middle finger back and place the bandaged cork against the knuckle.

❑ Hold the bandaged cork in place with fingers on either side.

❑ While trying to tie the ends of the cloth together with one hand say, "I cut my finger. Could you tie this bandage on for me?"

❑ When your helpful grandchild has hold of the bandage and starts to tie the knot, you pull your hand away, leaving him or her holding what at first appears to be the end of your finger.

❑ Say something like, "Oh, my *finger.*"

❑ Wait for a moment to let the child get the joke. Then explain what happened.

❑ Demonstrate. Have a good laugh.

❑ Give your grandchild the bandaged cork and let him or her play this joke on someone else.

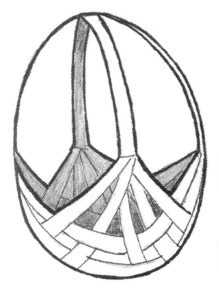

## MAY DAY

### Make your own
### May Basket

**Materials**: 2 sheets of 12" by 9" construction paper of different colors, stapler.

❑ Cut construction paper in strips one inch wide and 12 inches long.

❑ Place six strips of the same color on your work area.

❑ Weave five strips of the other color through the six strips.

❑ With Grandparent's help (four hands are needed), gather the ends of the six strips together and staple together.

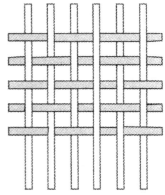

❑ Next gather the ends of the five strips and staple.

❑ Using two strips — double thickness – make a handle.

❑ Staple it across the top of the basket.

❑ Make another handle across the top of the basket in the opposite direction.

❑ Add flowers you pick from Grandparent's garden and you have a May basket to give to parents or a special friend or acquaintance.

## A SPECIAL FOURTH OF JULY

### Red, white and blue stars

**Materials:** Non-toxic, multi-purpose glue, red, blue and silver glitter.

❑ Draw stars with a glue bottle on waxed paper or heavy plastic food storage bags. Don't worry about making perfect stars (if it has five points it's a star).

❑ Make the glue lines thicker by going over them a second time.

❑ Wait about 2 hours and apply more glue, then sprinkle on the glitter and let dry. It will take about 24 hours for the stars to dry and harden.

❑ When the stars are hard gently peel away the waxed paper or plastic bag.

❑ Dampen the back with a moist paper towel and stick on windows or refrigerator.

### Hold your own
### flag-raising ceremony

Do you display the flag on Fourth of July? Then why not do it with a ceremony.

❑ Play a lively marching tune on your record, tape or CD player.

❑ While carrying the flag, march back and forth in front of your house.

❑ After saying the Pledge of Allegiance, place the flag in its holder.

This is fun, but remind your grandchild that it is also a way to show respect for our flag and country.

### Make a fun Fourth of July
### rocket balloon

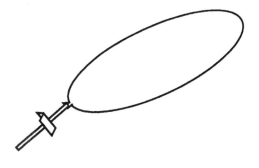

**Materials:** Long balloon (red, white or blue) rubber band, plastic drinking straw, 3" square of paper.

❑ Cut straw in half and insert one half into the other half to make a double thick straw.

❑ Slide the opening of the balloon over the end of the straw and secure with a rubber band.

❑ Make a fin by folding a 3" square of paper in half.

❑ With sharp end of a pencil make a hole in the center of the paper.

❑ Push the straw through this hole.

❑ Hold the balloon on the straw and inflate.

❑ Let it go!

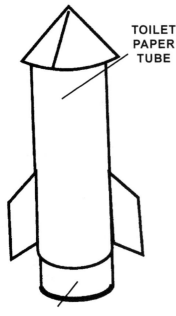

**TOILET PAPER TUBE**

**FILM CANISTER**

## Fourth of July Rocket

For an older grandchild, wanting more sophistication, here's another rocket.

**Materials:** Toilet paper tube, film canister, duct tape, construction paper, paint, fizzing antacid tablet (you know, the kind used for headaches, where you drop a tablet in a glass of water and it fizzes up).

❑ Cut straight up the side of the toilet paper tube.

❑ Lap the toilet paper tube around the film canister and tape securely. The snap-on lid must stick out of the tube at least ¼ inch.

❑ Make a nose cone and glue onto the end of the tube opposite the film canister.

❑ Add fins.

❑ Decorate the rocket.

❑ Put two teaspoons water in the film canister.

❑ Add a half seltzer tablet.

❑ Quickly snap on the lid.

❑ Set the rocket in launch position.

❑ Gas formed by the fizzing seltzer tablet builds pressure in the canister, pops the lid off and sends the rocket up.

❑ The tighter the lid fits the canister, the higher the rocket will go.

## WITCHES, GOBLINS AND JACK-O'-LANTERNS

### Halloween mobile

**Materials:** String, orange, black and white construction paper, black marker.

### Make a four-sided jack-o'-lantern

❑ Cut two orange circles 3 inches in diameter.
❑ Fold in half and staple the centers together on the fold.
❑ With marker make a jack-o'-lantern face on each of the four sides.

fold

### Make a witch's hat

❑ Fold black paper.
❑ Cut half a witch's hat on the fold.
❑ Unfold.

### Make a ghost

❑ Using two hands, tear a ghost shape.
❑ With black marker draw mouth and eyes.
❑ Why tear the ghost? Because ghosts do not have a well defined shape.

Now hang the jack-o'-lantern, witch's hat and ghost on a string and you have a simple one-string mobile.

## Scarecrow yard decoration

**Materials:** Old clothes, newspapers, stick, string, pumpkin.

❑ Stuff a pair of old pants and a shirt with crushed newspapers.

❑ Tuck the shirt into the top of the pants.

❑ Tie gloves on the sleeves and put old work shoes on the pant legs.

❑ Set the stick firmly in the ground and tie the stuffed clothes to it.

❑ Top this creation with a pumpkin head.

## Paper plate witch mask

**Materials:** Paper plate, black construction paper, brown, black or gray yarn, colored markers, string, glue.

❑ Hold paper plate to child's face and mark eyes, nose and mouth.

❑ Cut mouth, eyes and nose holes where you marked.

❑ Let your grandchild color the witch's face with markers.

Suggest black, pointy eyebrows, green lips and warts – of course.

❑ Help your grandchild cut a triangle hat out of black construction paper.

❑ Glue the black witch hat in place with yarn hair hanging out from under it.

❑ Punch holes under the "hair" on each side and thread string through the holes.

❑ Tie the mask on your grandchild's head.

❑ Put green eye shadow on your little witch's nose and she is ready for trick-or-treating.

### Pumpkin luminaries

**Materials:**  Lunch-size paper bags, sand, votive candles.

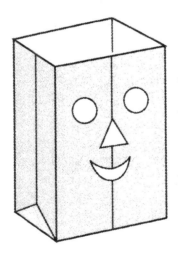

❑ Open paper bag and make a fold in the center of the front.

❑ Cut half a jack-o'-lantern nose and mouth on this fold.

❑ Punch a hole in the bag for the eyes and shape the hole with scissors.

❑ Put sand in the bottom of the sack – this gives a stable base in which to set a votive candle.

❑ On a frosty Halloween night, these paper-sack jack-o'-lanterns shining outside your windows will welcome trick-or-treaters with a warm glow.

---

**Warning:** Luminaries are a fire hazard. Set them away from curtains or draperies and maintain constant surveillance. Have a fire extinguisher handy.

---

## Cat's whiskers

**Material**: A piece of string about 4½ ft. long tied in a loop.

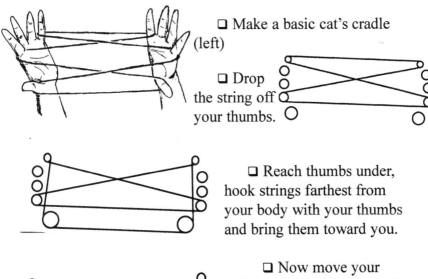

❑ Make a basic cat's cradle (left)

❑ Drop the string off your thumbs.

❑ Reach thumbs under, hook strings farthest from your body with your thumbs and bring them toward you.

❑ Now move your thumbs over one near string and under the next string. Pull up with hooked strings on your thumbs.

❑ Drop strings from little fingers.

❑ Use little fingers to go over string closest to the little finger and then under the next string.

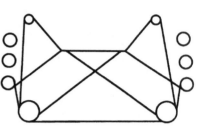

❑ Drop strings from thumbs.

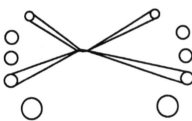

There you have it – *cat's whiskers.* If you don't believe it, hold the center of the configuration under your nose and look in the mirror.

## Witch's hat

❑ Start with the cat's whiskers to make a witch's hat.

❑ Make a cat's whiskers.

❑ Slide thumbs over two strings closest to your body and under the next strings.

❑ Pick up the top string in the middle where all the strings cross with your teeth. Pull up.

❑ Drop little fingers and keep pulling up.

Look in the mirror and you will see a *witch's hat.*

## Have a happy birthday party

Birthdays are generally celebrated in the child's own home, but should you be asked to provide the party, think of the successful parties you gave your children and plan accordingly.

There are lots of things to do and games to play. Games such as Drop the Handkerchief; Musical Chairs; and Button, Button, Who's Got the Button are as sure to please now as they were twenty years ago.

You can also:

❑ Make or buy party hats.
❑ Decorate with balloons, crepe paper and paper coils.
❑ Serve traditional cake and ice cream.
❑ Take lots of pictures or videotapes.

And don't forget the important traditions of singing Happy Birthday and blowing out the candles.

## A THANKSGIVING
## TO REMEMBER

Your grandchildren will enjoy the Thanksgiving feast and the pleasures of family togetherness, but it's what you do with them – not what they had to eat that they'll remember.

### Leaf raking fun

Sounds like work, doesn't it? But for grandkids who live in new neighborhoods with small young trees, this can be a real treat.

### Button hunting game

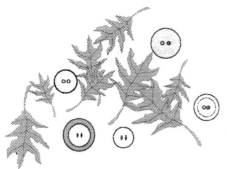

**Materials:** One dozen or more buttons. Pile of leaves.

❑ Rake up a big pile of leaves.
❑ Then players push the buttons one at a time deep

into the pile. After all the buttons have been hidden in the leaves the game begins.

❑ At a given signal the players dig into the pile to find the buttons.

❑ The winner, of course, is the player who finds the most buttons.

## Make leaf
## place mats

**Materials:** Leaves, 12" by 18" white paper, crayons.

❑ Gather a few leaves, arrange them on your work surface, place paper over the leaves and tape the paper so it won't move.

❑ Then rub the side of a crayon (wrapper removed) across the paper.

❑ Almost like magic the leaves appear on the white paper.

## Have messy fun
## with spatter prints

**Materials:** Poster paint, old toothbrush, screen, white paper, leaves.

❑ Cover the work area with old newspapers or old vinyl tablecloth.

❑ Arrange leaves on the white paper place mat.

❑ Dip toothbrush in paint (any color) and brush across screen held over the leaves.

❑ The paint will spatter.

❑ Let it dry.

❑ Lift off the leaves.

And there you have it: spatter prints. For fun, try different colors, and various types of leaves.

## A SPECIAL CHRISTMAS AT GRANDMA AND GRANDPA'S

Soon after you become grandparents, you discover that "I'll be home for Christmas," doesn't necessarily mean your house.

Young families have two sets of grandparents to consider when making holiday plans and they also want to establish their own Christmas traditions.

Suggest the family gather at your house once in awhile (maybe every five years). Then make *this* Christmas celebration a memorable event.

### Memorable Christmas suggestions

❑ Decorate the whole house. If grandchildren live nearby, let them help with things that are fun. Don't get upset if some decorations get broken. Save the pieces and glue them back together.

❑ Don't spend all your time in the kitchen. Cook a big meal every other day and on the other days snack on leftovers and make sandwiches.

❑ Remember Christmas is a time for renewing spiritual values and enjoying family togetherness. Plan activities that include everyone.

# Christmas activities

### Jigsaw puzzles

❑ Select two puzzles with a Christmas theme – one less than 100 pieces for little ones and one of 500 pieces or less for adults and older children.

### Play in the snow

There's lots of fun if you can go outside and play in the snow. You can have a snowball pitching contest (see who can hit a target) or get together to build an old-fashioned snowman.

If there is no snow in your front yard, you might be able to travel to nearby mountains for a day of sledding or skiing.

## Ice skating

Go to an indoor ice skating rink. This is better than skating outdoors on a pond because the ice is always safe and skates can be rented.

## Play your family's favorite
## card or board games

Gather around the table for a wild game of Monopoly or cards. Don't forget to serve popcorn.

## Ladies' shopping day

❑ Give each of the girls in your family some money and join the crowd at the mall. When you are under no pressure to buy, this can be fun. When you get tired, go home.

## Boys' afternoon
## at the golf course

While the ladies are shopping, the men can go golfing (if you live in a place where the sun shines).

## Play spin the dreidel

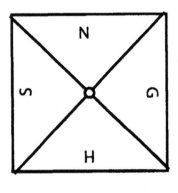

If you don't have a dreidel, it's easy to make one.

**Material:** 3" square of cardboard, pencil, marker.

❑ Draw a line from corner to corner on the square.
❑ Write a Hebrew letter (Nun, Gimmel, Heh, Shin) or N, G, H, S in each section.

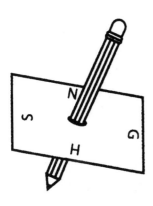

❑ Make a small hole in the center of the square and push a pencil through the hole.

The cardboard must fit tightly around the pencil and the point of the pencil should stick out about one inch.

## How to play the game

❑ Each player is given the same number of objects, such as pennies, candies, or nuts.

❑ The players put one of their objects into a pot and the first player spins the dreidel.

❑ If the dreidel stops with the N on top, the player takes nothing from the pot.

❑ If the dreidel stops with the G on top, the player takes the entire pot and all the other players put one object in the pot

❑ If the dreidel stops with the H on top, the player takes half the pot.

❑ If the dreidel stops with the S on top, the player puts one object into the pot.

❑ The game ends when one player has won everything.

## Go to church or synagogue

The holidays would not be complete without attending some religious service.

If you don't all belong to the same church, you can decide to go where the majority want to go.

If you can't agree to this plan, then go your separate ways, but do it respectfully.

## Make gingerbread persons

**Materials:** Gingerbread cookie recipe, things normally found in Grandma's kitchen.

### Gingerbread persons recipe

Ingredients:
¾ cup heavy cream, whipped
1¼ cups dark-brown sugar
½ cup molasses
1 tablespoon baking soda
1½ teaspoon ginger
1½ teaspoon grated lemon rind
4½ cups sifted flour

Stir together first six ingredients until well blended. Then stir in flour. Roll out dough on lightly floured surface until it is about 1/8 inch thick.

❑ Cut out gingerbread persons with cookie cutter or make original shapes with sharp knife.

❑ Bake in 300-degree oven for 10 to 15 minutes.

❑ After baked and cooled, decorate with confectioners' icing. Use an icing tube or make your own tube from sturdy paper rolled into a cone and fastened with tape.

## Make a decoration

**Materials:** Construction paper, string.

This is an easy-to-make, festive-looking decoration.
- ❑ Cut a round circle out of construction paper – any size, any color.
- ❑ Start at the edge and cut a spiral into the center. (Like peeling an apple.)
- ❑ Punch a hole in the center and hang.

**Optional:** Decorate with glitter.

The coil will turn with the air currents in the room.

## Read or tell a favorite Christmas story

One member of the family can read aloud or everyone might take turns reading or telling about a Christmas experience.

Grandma or Grandpa might remember Christmas in "the good old days." The kids can tell their own favorite Christmas stories.

It's fun to tape the reading for future listening.

### Hang stockings and get ready
### for a visit from St. Nicholas

Grandpa or a favorite uncle might want to play Santa for the small grandchildren.

## How to play Santa

One year our Uncle Chuck staged a visit from St. Nicholas for the grandchildren.

On Christmas Eve, Chuck rang sleigh bells outside. When everyone ran out to see Santa, Chuck and I quickly filled the stockings and made footprints on the carpet in front of the fireplace with a stencil and spray snow.

Of course, Santa was not found outside, but when everyone came back in the house, they found filled stocking and snowy footprints – proof that Santa had been there.

Incidentally, the spray snow did not stain the carpet and was easy to clean up.

## DEVELOPING FAMILY TRADITIONS

Developing unique family traditions is part of the pleasure of holiday celebrations. However, family traditions cannot be planned. Enjoy your family and your grandchildren and the traditions will evolve naturally.

## KEEPING FAMILY TRADITIONS ALIVE

Record what you do in a special scrapbook, year by year, complete with photographs. Date it and tell who is there, their age, something about each of them, and what you ate and did.

Perhaps you can write down what gifts each person received at Christmas.

Each time the family gathers at Christmas, you can look at your own personal Christmas book. This will become a special keepsake for your family.

## HELPING WELCOME A NEW BABY

Sometimes grandchildren are scheduled to visit grandparents when the new baby is due to arrive. But more often, grandparents are asked to be baby sitters, taking care of the children in their own home.

If you are invited to visit while Mommy goes to the hospital, put a toy or two in your suitcase for the grandchild or grandchildren. This is the time when older children sometimes feel left out, so give them a little gift and plan some activities to make them feel special and important.

It is best, if your suitcase will hold them, to bring materials needed for activities with you.

### Make a "welcome baby" sign

You and the grandkids can get together to plan a big or large welcoming sign for the new baby. The making of the sign can be fun, and, it gives everyone a chance to show their feelings for the new member of the family.

**Materials:** Roll of butcher paper or brown wrapping paper, poster paint or water-soluble markers, duct tape.

❑ Roll out enough butcher paper or wrapping paper to reach across the front of your outside garage door. Tape the ends down so you can work on the surface easily.

❑ The grandkids can paint in large letters: "WELCOME TO OUR FAMILY."

❑ You might add the baby's name to this message.

❑ For better size and spacing, Grandma could pencil in the letters and let grandchildren paint them.

❑ Next tape the sign to the garage door. Now everyone will know that a new baby is welcome in this home.

### Baby's room mobile

This is a fun gift the brother or sister can make for the new baby.

**Materials:** Clothes hanger, construction paper, crayons, water-soluble markers or colored pencils, string.

❑ Draw and color five or six interesting shapes on construction paper – fish or birds for example.

❑ Cut out shapes.

❑ With long and short lengths of string hang shapes from clothes hanger.

❑ Hang over baby's crib where baby can see it. From time to time make it move lightly to catch baby's eye. Maybe you can croon to baby at the same time.

> **Warning:** Grandma or Grandpa should check to make certain the shapes and the mobile are securely fastened and cannot accidentally be knocked down or fall into the crib.

# 7

# Meet two super grandparents

BILL AND GAI CUSICK, who live in Salt Lake City, Utah, have eighteen grandchildren. Because of their special vision and activities, they deserve the title of "super grandparents."

In1988, they purchased a special summer home, "a Grandma House," in a near-by rural town where their grand-kids could visit and enjoy themselves.

The "Grandma House" was more than a hundred years old and where other buyers might have seen old, dilapidated barns and chicken coops that would have to be torn down, Bill and

Gai saw clubhouses, forts and playhouses. With four bed-
rooms the house had plenty of room for all the grandkids. On
an acre of ground in a town of less than 700 people, it was the
perfect grandparent's summer home.

Gai says, "We've had as many as twelve here at once,
twelve grandkids."

She laughs and adds, "It gets real crazy!"

### Tree houses & a "bean house"

Grandkids are always involved in big construction projects. The first year, a nine-year old grandson talked his unmar-
ried uncle into helping him build a tree house in an apple tree.

The next year an older grandchild built another tree house
in a bigger tree.

Several years ago, the youngest granddaughters turned a
brooder house into a playhouse.

Another project was the bean house. Gai tells how she
found the former owner's old beanpoles in a far corner of the
back yard. She tied them together like a teepee and planted
beans around them.

That was the beginning of the bean house. Every year, the
bean house is remodeled and improved.

Creative play is encouraged. Grandchildren write and produce their own plays – usually an adaptation of a well known
fairy tale. A bedspread hung over a wire across the porch
makes a stage and Grandma is an uncritical audience.

The granddaughters like to dress-up in Gai's old square
dance dresses, don sunbonnets and pretend they are pioneers.

An old farm wagon with the aid of the children's imaginations becomes a prairie schooner and has — without moving
from the shelter of an old corral fence — made countless trips
across the continent.

Do Grandma and Grandpa Cusick have rules?  Yes.

The first rule is: Everybody plays together. This rule
became necessary when Gai discovered one child paring up
with another and excluding a third child.

Another rule is the kids can't bring money to spend. If they want to go to the store, they must earn the money. Gai gives them jobs picking up rocks, washing her car or sweeping the walks.

Kids are not allowed to watch TV at Grandma and Grandpa Cusick's.

Grandkids are expected to make their beds and clean up "their stuff." But Grandma doesn't expect perfection.

### No "I'm bored"

And last, but not least, they are not allowed to say, "I'm bored."

The kids made a chart of twenty-three things they can do. The list starts with "Hide & Seek" and ends with "Clean Front Room." When grandchildren ask what they can do, Gai points to the list hanging on the kitchen wall.

Both Gai and Bill have a good sense of humor. Things that might upset other grandparents become family jokes at the Cusick's.

Three years ago a nine-year-old grandson and his friend chose "Drive lawn mower" from the list of things to do. (This means ride the mower, not mow the lawn.) They hit a high-center and tore the bottom out of the mower. Bill growled about their careless driving, and after the boys went home, he fixed the lawn mower.

On their next visit Grandpa greeted them with a grin and asked, "Did you get a driver's license yet?"

### Some final thoughts

Okay, so Bill and Gai Cusick are super grandparents. But what about grandparents who live in a city, who don't have barns, sheds and chicken coops – not to mention tree houses and old farm wagons?

Any house, anywhere, can be a "Grandma House." You don't have to move or buy another house. You don't have to have a big lot, or trees, or sheds.

All you really need is love and activities and projects – things found in this book.

A friend once told me "The secret to being a good grandmother is having good grandchildren."

While this is true, I also believe the secret to having good grandchildren is being a good grandparent. This takes a little effort, but it will give you and your grandkids real pleasure and create wonderful memories.

# Grandma and Grandpa's record & memory section of activities with grandkids

Here you can record all the activities
and fun times you've had together

**Activity**                                                  **Date**

_____

_____

_____

_____

_____

_____

_____

_____

_____

Activity                                                    Date

Activity                                    Date

_____

_____

_____

_____

_____

_____

_____

_____

_____

_____

_____

_____

_____

Activity                                             Date

Activity                                                    Date
_____

_____

_____

_____

_____

_____

_____

_____

_____

_____

_____

_____

_____

Activity                                                    Date

# Index

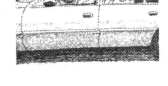

# R

# S

# T

# V

# W

# Z

*Grandpa and Grandma Luttrell and grandkids Kevin, Jessica and Miss Jenn display the gingerbread house they created together. Kevin (left) shows off his face painting, a Santa hat.*

## About the author

Jean Luttrell is a retired third grade teacher. During her 37 years in the classroom, she acquired child management skills and accumulated directions for many practical hands-on activities for use with children. When their oldest grandchild, Jess, came for a visit in 1986, the author was ready with games and ideas to make the visit fun for both grandparent and grandchild. Later, when Kevin and Miss Jenn, the second and third grandchildren, came for visits, Jean's bags of tricks expanded to include activities for both boys and girls and children of all ages. Over the years, Jean has found what works and what doesn't and has adapted the projects and games she used as a teacher to fit her needs as an active grandparent. Jean and husband, Ben, live in Boulder City, Nevada. Three years ago, they purchased a second home, a "Grandma House," located near their grandchildren in Dammeron Valley, Utah.

The book's illustrator, Chuck Luttrell, is the author's son and the grandchildren's favorite uncle. Chuck lives in Boulder City with his wife, Eileen, and their cat, William Wallace.